MAKING CLASSIC WOODEN TOYS

21 Step-by-Step Projects

EDITED BY
SCOTT FRANCIS

POPULAR WOODWORKING BOOKS

CINCINNATI, OHIO

popularwoodworking.com

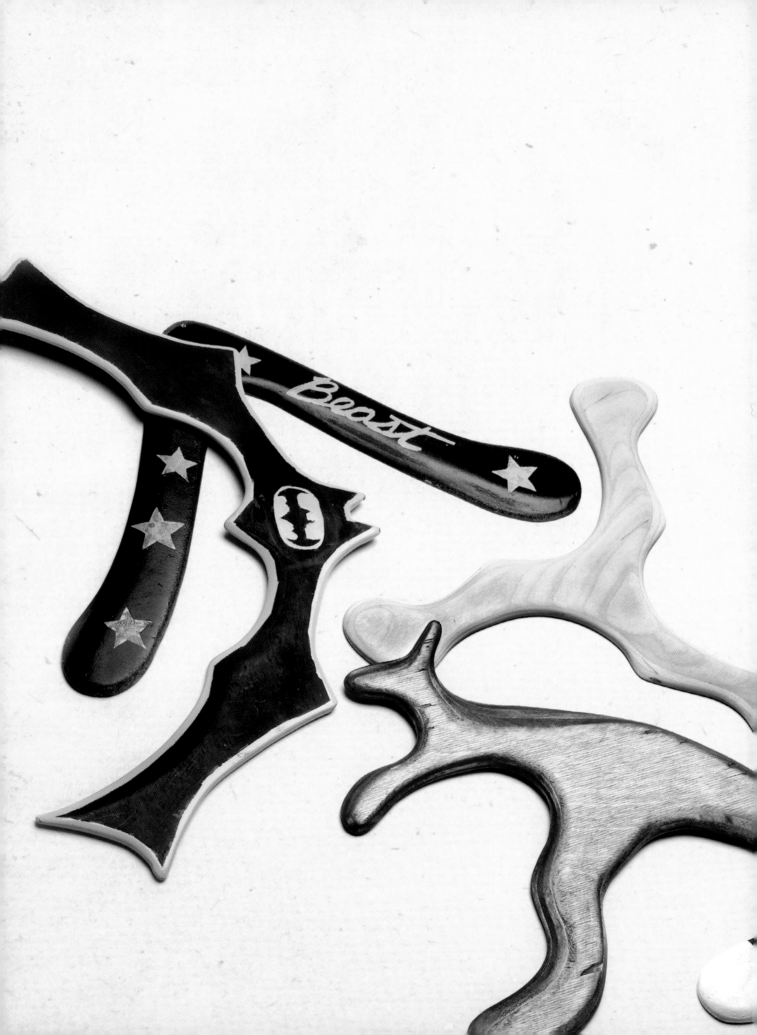

MAKING CLASSIC WOODEN TOYS

21 Step-by-Step Projects

EDITED BY
SCOTT FRANCIS

CONTENTS

FUN FURNITURE

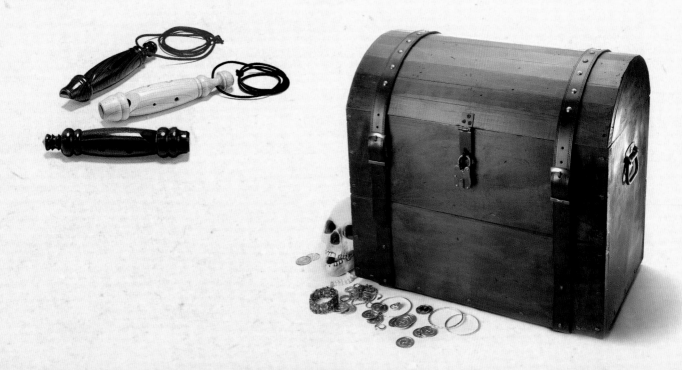

INTRODUCTION

Perhaps it's because I've become a father myself – or maybe it's just a sign of getting older – but I've found myself thinking fondly of old toys. I'm not talking about the Transformers, Stretch Armstrongs and Star Wars figures of my youth (though, I love those toys with all my heart). Those kinds of toys are special in their own way with their wonderfully cheap plastic and bright colors, but I'm talking about handcrafted toys – the toys you play with when you visit your grandfather.

My own grandpa had a workshop. He had a lathe and used it to make all kinds of stuff. In fact, when we went to visit we hardly ever saw my grandpa because he spent all of his time in the shop, only coming in the house for a quick dinner before returning to his work (he was an engineer). He didn't spend much time with us kids, but we knew him by the toys he made. I remember playing with a huge bin of homemade Lincoln-style logs that he'd crafted. They were the first thing my little sister and I dug out whenever we went to visit. But there were other things: wooden games with marbles, peg games, carved snakes that wriggled on hinges, wooden race cars powered by rubber bands, spinning tops and strange whiligigs. These toys were all over my grandmother's house – and I say "grandmother's house" because I'm very serious when I say my grandfather pretty much lived in his workshop. His wooden toys held a fascination for me because they were so different than the plastic sheen of my everyday toys. Even as a kid I sensed that these toys were something special. We were careful when we played with them. Those old toys were, in a word, charming.

My grandfather never invited me into his shop to show me how he made the toys. I guess he thought me too young at the time, and I suppose I had other things on my mind – like Star Wars. If I had it to do over, I would have asked him to teach me, but sadly he passed away before I ever had that notion. But whenever I see handmade toys I think of him in his shop making whatever popped into his head.

This collection of wooden toys represents the kind of charm I'm talking about. Chosen from pieces that have appeared in past issues of *Popular Woodworking Magazine* and *American Woodworker*, these puzzles, toys and games are full of nostalgia and similar designs have been played with by children for generations.

Put simply, wooden toys stand the test of time. Perhaps this book will remind you of a beloved toy from your own childhood – and inspire you to make a handmade toy for a kid you love.

—*Scott Francis, Editor*

PUZZLES

CHAPTER ONE

WOODEN BURR PUZZLES

by Jock Holmen

Something's got to give when pieces of wood intersect at 90° angles. That's the reality behind the curious assemblies shown here. Known as burr puzzles, because they resemble seed burrs, these brainteasers consist of three or more notched pieces that go together at right angles. Give one of these tricksters to an unsuspecting friend and watch the fun. Disassembling each puzzle is the easy part. Putting the pieces back together is the real challenge!

Precision is the key to making the puzzles work effectively. Each part must be accurately marked, milled and cut.

The first step for all three puzzles is to mill long ¾" x ¾" blanks. Use a caliper to measure the thicknesses precisely and make sure the blanks are square. Then cut the individual puzzle pieces to exact length from the blanks.

A shop-made jig makes it easy to notch the pieces for all three puzzles on the table saw, using a dado set (**Fig. A**, on page 12). This jig consists of a sled with runners, a clamp and a fence. The runners fit the saw's miter slots, so the sled makes perpendicular cuts. For clean, tear-out-free results, a portion of the jig should be dedicated to each notch size. If, as shown, the blade is offset between the runners, you can use both sides of the sled. The jig's wide fence houses the dado set from both directions, for safety. Stop-blocks and spacers precisely position the pieces, so the notches (dados, actually) are accurately cut. Like the puzzle pieces themselves, the spacers must be precisely cut. To set up the jig, clamp one stop-block to the right of the slot (the exact distance – called the "jig set-up dimension" – depends on the puzzle you're creating). Use a puzzle piece and the spacers to locate and clamp the other stop. After you've installed each piece, secure it with the toggle clamp before you cut the dado (see Source, page 16).

The dados have to fit perfectly, so always make extra puzzle pieces, and start by making test cuts. Testing the dado widths and depths is pretty easy, because most of the pieces go together with lap joints. When the dados fit snugly, their widths are correct; when the joint surfaces are flush, the dado depths are correct. The pieces will go together more easily if you lightly sand their edges. That's it; you're ready to go.

THE THREE PIECE BURR

In appearance, this puzzle is my favorite, because of its perfect, simple symmetry. It's the only puzzle of the, three that requires cutting dados in two sizes (see **Fig. B**, on page 12).

Make the pieces

1. Cut 2¼" blocks from square ¾" stock, including extras for test cuts.
2. Set up the saw and the jig to cut ⅜" x ⅜" dados.
3. Clamp the jig's right stop-block 1⅛" from the edge of the ⅜" slot.
4. Snug a test piece and both ⅜" spacers against the right stop. Butt the left stop-block against the spacers and clamp it.
5. Cut dados in a couple test pieces. Fit them together to check the dados' width and depth; make necessary adjustments.
6. Install Piece A and cut the first dado (**Photo 1**).
7. Rotate Piece A, reposition the spacers and cut the second dado (**Photo 2**).
8. Turn the jig end for end and set it up to cut ⅜" x ¾" dados.
9. Clamp the right stop-block 1⅛" from the edge of the ¾" slot.
10. Repeat Steps 4 and 5.
11. Install Piece B with one spacer at each end. Cut the first dado (**Photo 3**).
12. Install Piece C and repeat Step 11.
13. Rotate Piece C one-quarter turn toward the dado set and cut the second dado.
14. Reinstall Piece B and repeat Step 13.
15. Ease the corners of the bridge on Piece C to create an octagon.

Fig. A. Dadoing jig

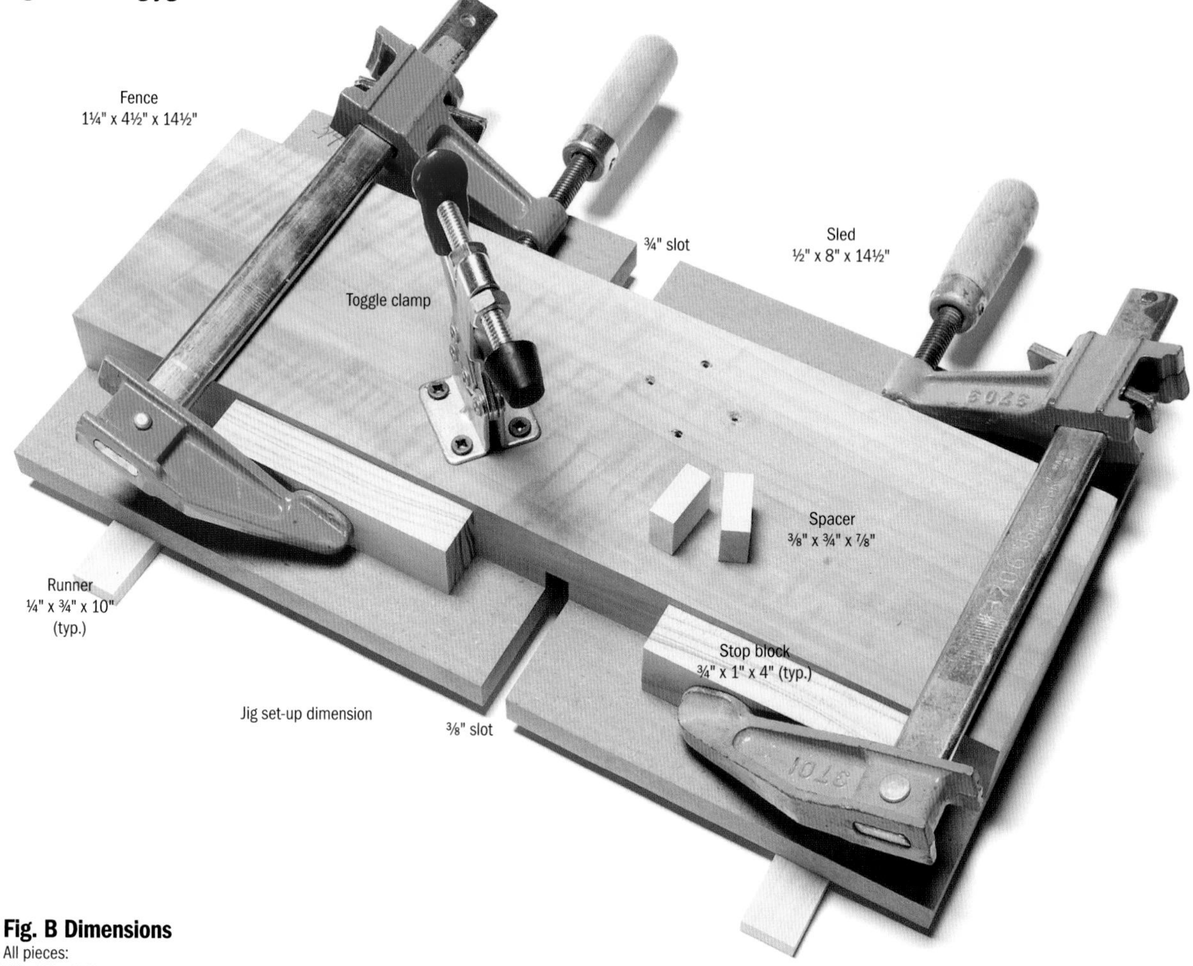
Fence
1¼" x 4½" x 14½"
Toggle clamp
¾" slot
Sled
½" x 8" x 14½"
Spacer
⅜" x ¾" x ⅞"
Runner
¼" x ¾" x 10"
(typ.)
Stop block
¾" x 1" x 4" (typ.)
Jig set-up dimension
⅜" slot

Fig. B Dimensions

All pieces:
¾" x ¾" x 2¼"

Jig set-up
Dimension: 1⅛"

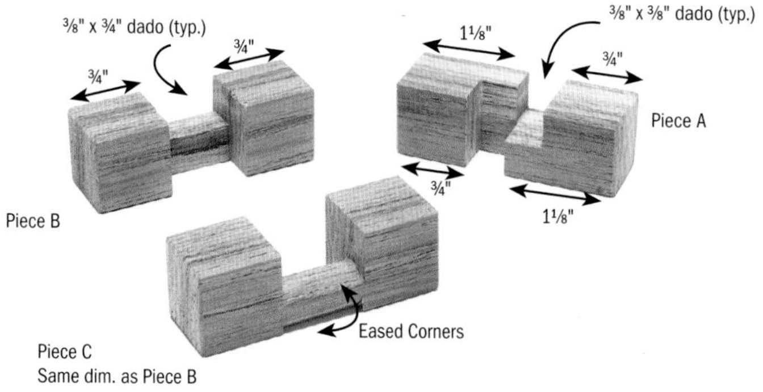
⅜" x ¾" dado (typ.)
¾"
¾"
Piece B
1⅛"
⅜" x ⅜" dado (typ.)
¾"
Piece A
¾"
1⅛"
Eased Corners
Piece C
Same dim. as Piece B

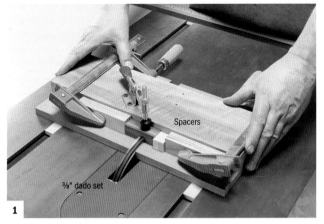

1

Cut a ⅜" x ⅜" dado after clamping the stop-blocks in position and installing Piece A with both spacers to the left.

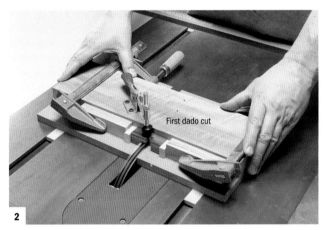

2

Cut a second dado in Piece A after rotating it one-quarter turn toward the dado set and reinstalling it with one spacer at each end.

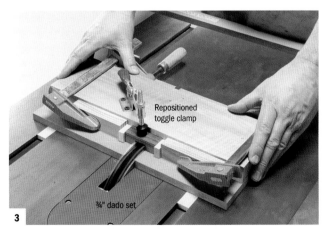

3

Use the opposite side of the jig to cut ¾" wide dados in Pieces B and C. Cut the first dado, rotate each piece one-quarter turn toward the dado set, and then cut a second dado. Make these cuts with one spacer installed at each end.

Assemble the puzzle

1. Connect Pieces A and C.
2. Install Piece B from the top.
3. Rotate Piece C one-quarter turn.

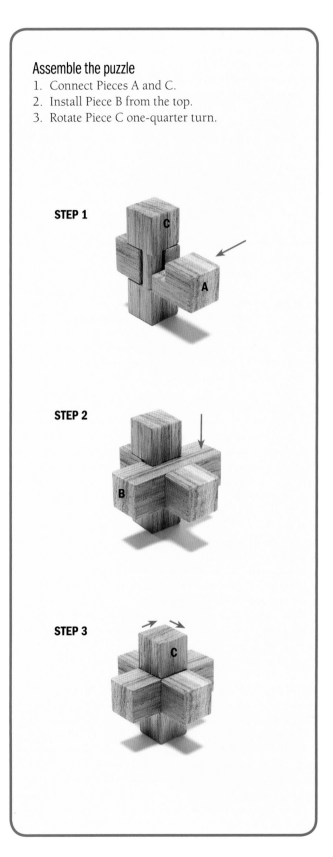

STEP 1

STEP 2

STEP 3

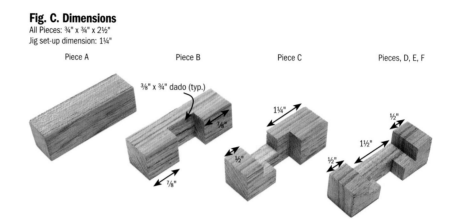

Fig. C. Dimensions
All Pieces: ¾" x ¾" x 2½"
Jig set-up dimension: 1¼"

Piece A   Piece B   Piece C   Pieces, D, E, F

⅜" x ¾" dado (typ.)
⅞"
⅞"
1¼"
½"
½"
1½"
½"

THE SIX PIECE BURR

By all accounts, this burr is the most well known, because the six pieces can be notched in so many different ways and still assembled to create the same form.

Make the pieces

1. Cut 2½" long blocks from square ¾" stock, including extras for test cuts (**Fig. C**, above).
2. Set up the saw and the jig to cut ⅜" x ¾" dados.
3. Clamp the jig's right stop-block 1¼" from the edge of the ¾" slot.
4. Snug a ⅜" spacer against the right stop, followed by a test piece and the remaining ⅜" spacer. Butt and clamp the left stop-block against the spacer.

5. Cut dados in a couple test pieces. Fit them together to check the dados' width and depth, and make necessary adjustments.
6. Set aside Piece A; it's already done.
7. To complete Piece B, install it in the jig with a spacer at each end and cut a dado.
8. Repeat Step 7, using Pieces C, D, E and F.
9. To complete Piece C, rotate it one-quarter turn toward the dado set. Install it with both spacers to the left and cut a second dado.
9. Repeat Step 8, using Pieces D, E and F. Complete these pieces by moving both spacers to the right and cutting a third dado.

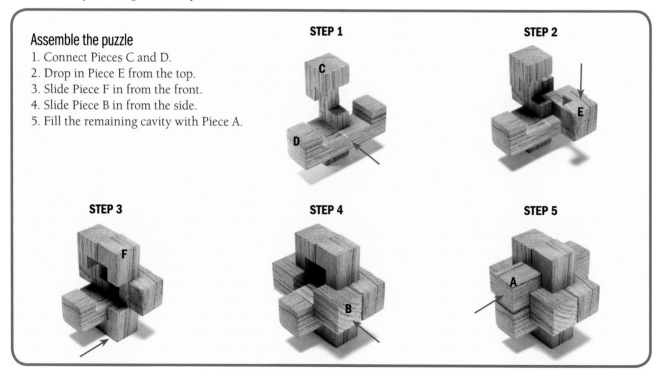

Assemble the puzzle

1. Connect Pieces C and D.
2. Drop in Piece E from the top.
3. Slide Piece F in from the front.
4. Slide Piece B in from the side.
5. Fill the remaining cavity with Piece A.

STEP 1

STEP 2

STEP 3

STEP 4

STEP 5

THE TWELVE PIECE BURR

A good nickname for this puzzle is "The Intimidator," because all 12 pieces are identical and taking the puzzle apart is as confounding as putting it together.

Make the pieces

1. Cut 4½" long blocks from square ¾" stock, including extras for test cuts (**Fig D**, right).
2. Make a pair of ¾" x ¾" x ⅞" spacers.
3. Set up the saw and the jig to cut ⅜" x ¾" dados.
4. Clamp the jig's right stop-block 1⅞" from the edge of the ¾" slot.
5. Snug a ¾" spacer against the right stop, followed by a test piece and the other ¾" spacer. Butt and clamp the left stop-block against the spacer.
6. Cut dados in a couple test pieces. Fit them together to check the dados' width and depth, and make necessary adjustments.
7. Cut this dado in all 12 pieces.
8. Flip the piece end for end and reinstall it between the two spacers. Cut a second dado in all 12 pieces. Both dados should be in the same face.
9. Rotate the piece one-quarter turn toward the dado set and reinstall it with both ¾" spacers on the left. Cut this dado in all 12 pieces. This last cut creates a tab, which can be used to help assemble the puzzle.

Fig.D dimensions
All pieces: ¾" x ¾" x 4½"
Jig set-up dimension: 1⅞"

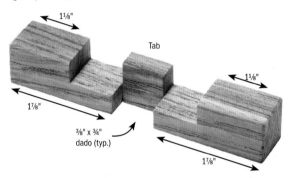

1⅛"

Tab

1⅛"

1⅞"

1⅞"

⅜" x ¾"
dado (typ.)

Assemble the puzzle

1. Assemble four pieces to form a tic-tac-toe grid. Orient two vertical pieces with their tabs on the right and facing to the front. Then install the two horizontal pieces with their tabs on the inside and facing to the back. A rectangular space should appear in the center.
2. Install the next two pieces with their tabs on the left and facing up. Slide one piece in from the left side and lock it around the vertical piece. Slide the second piece halfway through the rectangular space from the front. Then move it to the right, to lock around the other vertical piece.

STEP 1

Tab

STEP 2

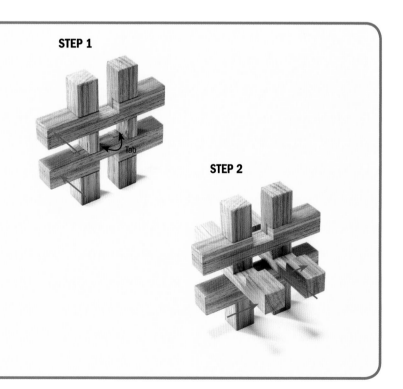

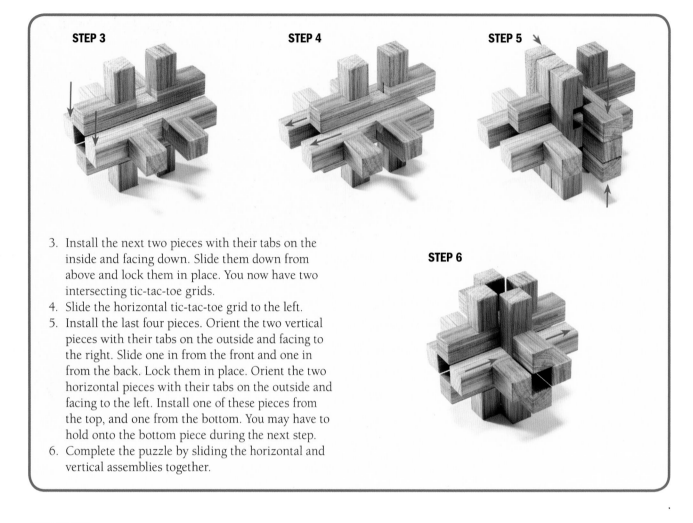

STEP 3

STEP 4

STEP 5

STEP 6

3. Install the next two pieces with their tabs on the inside and facing down. Slide them down from above and lock them in place. You now have two intersecting tic-tac-toe grids.
4. Slide the horizontal tic-tac-toe grid to the left.
5. Install the last four pieces. Orient the two vertical pieces with their tabs on the outside and facing to the right. Slide one in from the front and one in from the back. Lock them in place. Orient the two horizontal pieces with their tabs on the outside and facing to the left. Install one of these pieces from the top, and one from the bottom. You may have to hold onto the bottom piece during the next step.
6. Complete the puzzle by sliding the horizontal and vertical assemblies together.

SOURCE

Woodcraft
www.woodcraft.com, (800) 225-1153,
Toggle Clamp, #143938, $11.99.

CHAPTER TWO

ENIGMA CUBE

by Tom Caspar

How does it come apart? You'll be asked this question each time you hand one of these cubes to a friend. You'll answer, "Well, you just hold it like this, then pull." Your ability to read wood grain will help you to quickly identify which sides to grab. Your friend will be mystified.

That's just one of the small pleasures in making these airy nothings. They really don't have a purpose other than to tickle your fancy.

Start with a strip of wood that's ⅛" or ¼" thick, 2½" to 3" wide and 24" long. Its edges must be straight and parallel. I used spalted maple, but any wood will do. Although you can certainly mill the wood yourself, it's much easier to buy pieces that are precut to these dimensions.

Draw a long triangle on the strip before cutting it into pieces. This mark will help you reassemble the pieces in the same order later on. Install a crosscut blade in your saw, then cut the strip into pieces that are precisely square (**Photos 1** and **2**).

Set up the saw for cutting miters around all four sides of each piece (**Photos 3, 4** and **5**). Switch to a general purpose or combination blade. This is a finicky operation – I found that riding the pieces on a stout support board worked best. My board is held in place with a locking bar borrowed from a featherboard.

You might think that the pieces should have sharp edges when you're done, but that's not practical on pieces this small. As you push each piece past the blade, a sharp edge would dive right into the kerf in the subfence, ruining each cut. It's far better to leave a blunt edge, one that's only about ¹⁄₆₄" wide. Sneak up on this setting, moving the fence a little bit farther from the blade each time (this widens the cut). The best strategy is to remove half of the waste first on each piece, then gradually move the fence away from the blade, make a cut, and see how close you get to the goal.

Arrange the pieces back in order, then tape them together (**Photo 6**). Wax the inside faces and outside miters – this makes removing glue squeeze-out much easier during assembly. Glue the inside miters, then slide the cube together and tape it shut (**Photos 7, 8** and **9**). Wait overnight, then remove the tape and sand the cube's corners and faces.

You'll probably have to make a few practice cubes to master the technique, but if all has gone well, the cube's joints will be invisible – and it will slide apart with a most satisfying sound.

1

Set up a stop-block for cutting the cube's pieces from one long strip. Cut the first piece about ¼" extra long, then turn it sideways to position the block.

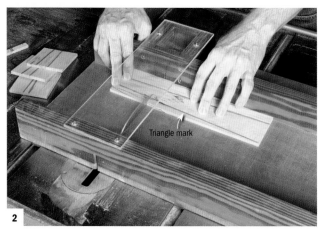

2

Cut the strip into six pieces. The strip is marked with a long, tapering triangle so you can reassemble the pieces in the correct order later on.

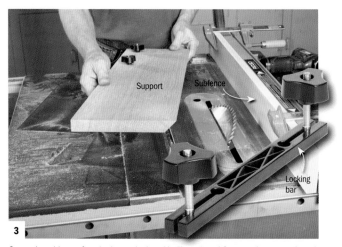

3

Set up the table saw for mitering each piece. You'll need a subfence and a support board. A locking bar that nests in the saw's miter slot prevents the support from sliding.

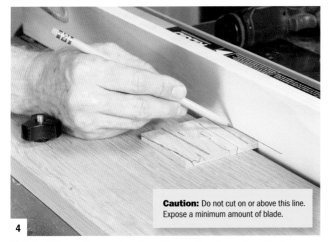

Caution: Do not cut on or above this line. Expose a minimum amount of blade.

4

Mark the thickness of your stock on the subfence. Adjust the position of the fence so the blade, tilted to 45°, cuts a hair below this line.

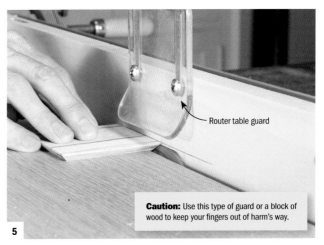

Router table guard

Caution: Use this type of guard or a block of wood to keep your fingers out of harm's way.

5

Saw all four edges of each piece. You don't want these miters to come to a sharp point – a very narrow, uncut edge should remain.

6

Arrange the pieces in the correct order, then divide them into two sets of three. Align the edges of each set against a block, then tape the pieces together.

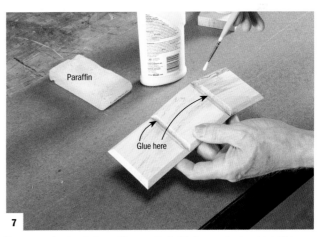

Paraffin

Glue here

7

Turn over each set and rub paraffin wax on the inside faces and outer edges of the three pieces. Apply glue on the edges that are taped together.

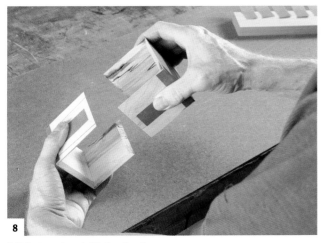

8

Fold the two sets and slide them together.

9

Tape the cube shut, so all the joints are tight. Let the glue cure overnight, then see if you can figure out how it comes apart!

CHAPTER THREE
ALPHABET PUZZLE

by Jock Holmen

Think twice before you take this puzzle apart. It has six faces, each face has nine squares and each square is lettered. That's two complete alphabets on 12 interlocked parts, all of which are duplicates but one. Having so many duplicates means each part can go almost anywhere. But because of the letters, each part can go in only one spot.

Making this puzzle may be easier than solving it, and once you're set up, you might as well make multiples. Just think, give a puzzle to each of your (highly motivated and inquisitive) kids, and the house will be quiet for the first time in months!

MAKE THE PARTS

1. Mill long ¾" x ¾" blanks that are absolutely square.
2. Cut the blanks to length to make the 12 parts (**Fig. B**), including extras for test cuts.
3. Set up the saw and the jig to cut ⅜" x ¾" dados.
4. To make Part A, install the wide spacers and cut a dado in a 1½" blank (**Photo 1**).
5. Switch to the narrow spacers and cut the dados in nine of the 2¼" blanks (**Photo 2**). Set five of these pieces aside as Parts B.

6. Cut a second dado in the other four pieces to make Parts C (**Photo 3**).
7. Use one wide spacer to cut wide dados in the remaining two blanks to make Parts D (**Photo 4**).
8. Very lightly sand the edges and ends of all 12 parts to create the tiny reveals that define the squares when the puzzle is assembled.
9. Scribe the middle square on the outside face of all Parts B and D (**Photo 5**).
10. Cut V-grooves on all Parts B and D to mimic the sanded reveals (**Photo 6**).

ASSEMBLE THE PUZZLE

1. Make three crosses with A and B parts.
2. Slide the crosses together.
3. Install Parts C.
4. Slide in Parts D.

Without letters, this puzzle is pretty easy to solve. Using different types of wood (Photo, page 20, top left) is one way to way to jazz it up. Adding numbers makes solving it quite a bit more difficult. But adding 27 different charac-

Fig. A Shop-made Jig

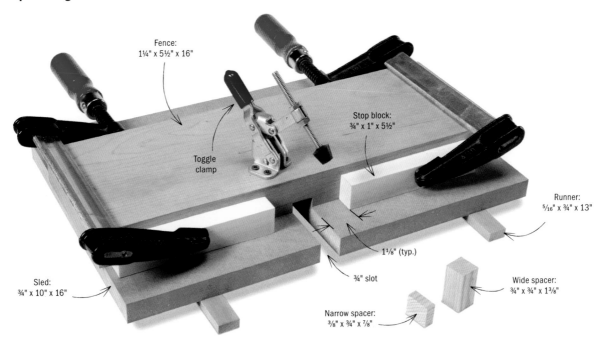

Fence:
1¼" x 5½" x 16"

Stop block:
¾" x 1" x 5½"

Toggle clamp

Runner:
⁵⁄₁₆" x ¾" x 13"

1⅛" (typ.)

¾" slot

Sled:
¾" x 10" x 16"

Wide spacer:
¾" x ¾" x 1³⁄₈"

Narrow spacer:
³⁄₈" x ¾" x ⅞"

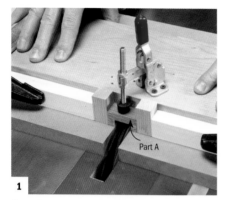

1 Create Part A by cutting a centered dado in the short blank after installing the wide spacers on both sides.

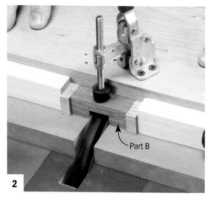

2 Create Part B by cutting a centered dado in nine of the long blanks after installing the two narrow spacers.

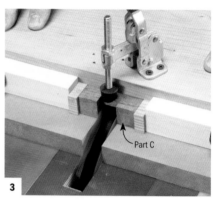

3 Create Part C by rotating four of the Part B blanks 90° toward the blade and cutting another centered dado.

Fig. B Dimensions
All parts ¾" x ¾"

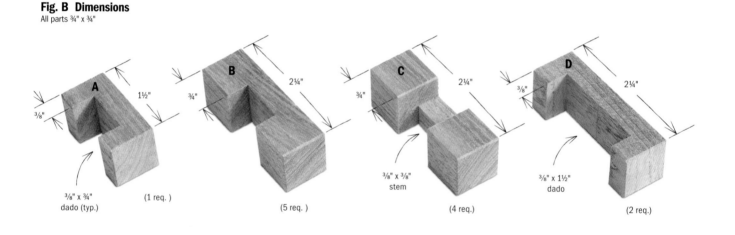

A 1½" ³⁄₈" ³⁄₈" x ¾" dado (typ.) (1 req.)

B 2¼" ¾" (5 req.)

C 2¼" ¾" ³⁄₈" x ³⁄₈" stem (4 req.)

D 2¼" ³⁄₈" ³⁄₈" x 1½" dado (2 req.)

ters (26 letters and a question mark) creates the ultimate challenge, especially if their orientation changes on each face. Carving or routing the characters is one option – the puzzle featured on page 20, (bottom left) was CNC-routed. You could also use stamps or stencils or peel-and-stick characters – a single $5 package of ½" letters and numerals (available at office supply stores) allows making four alphabet puzzles and two number puzzles.

For this puzzle to work properly, each part must be accurately milled and cut. If the joints are too tight, the puzzle won't go together; if the parts fit too loosely, it will fall apart. So, anytime you see a dimension in these instructions, add the word "precisely" before it.

Dados lock the parts together to form the cube. A shop-made jig makes it easy to cut them (**Fig. A**, page 21). This jig consists of a sled with runners, a clamp and

a fence. The runners fit the table saw's miter slots, so the sled makes perpendicular cuts. The wide fence houses the saw's dado set, for safety. Stop-blocks and spacers precisely position the puzzle parts, so the dados are accurately cut. Like the puzzle parts, the spacers must be precisely cut.

To set up the jig, clamp the stop-blocks 1⅛" from the slot on both sides. Then install the appropriate spacers and secure the puzzle part with the toggle clamp. The dados have to fit perfectly, so always make extra parts and start by making test cuts. Testing the dado widths and depths is pretty easy, because most of the parts go together with lap joints. When the dados fit snugly, their widths are correct; when the surfaces of the assembled joint are flush, the dado depths are correct. That's it; you're ready to go.

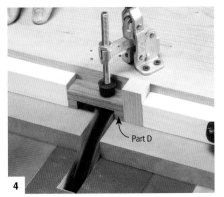

4

Create Part D by cutting a pair of dados in the remaining two blanks. Cut the first dado with the wide spacer on one side and the second with it on the other side.

5

Divide the face of each long part into three squares. Scribe each line after installing another dadoed part flush with the end to use as a straightedge.

6

Mimic three separate parts by inserting a bevel-edge chisel in each scribed line and tapping it once with a mallet to create a V-groove.

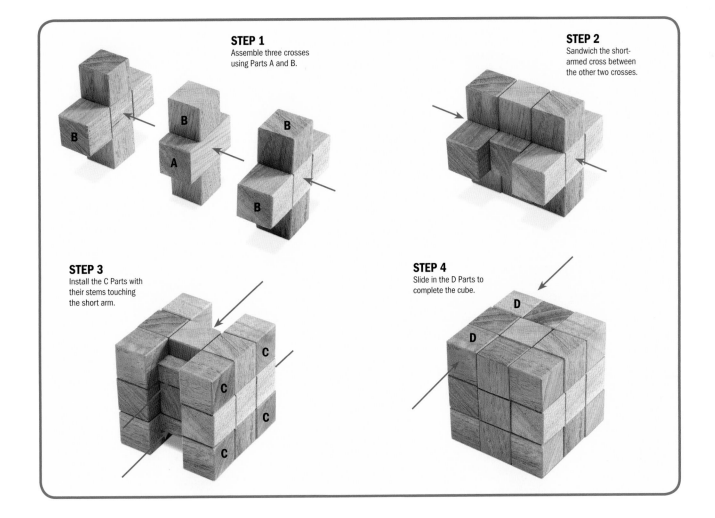

STEP 1
Assemble three crosses using Parts A and B.

STEP 2
Sandwich the short-armed cross between the other two crosses.

STEP 3
Install the C Parts with their stems touching the short arm.

STEP 4
Slide in the D Parts to complete the cube.

CHAPTER FOUR
MARBLE MAZE

by Joe Hurst-Wajszczuk

As one of the newest members of the Colorado Woodworkers' Guild, I wanted to build something special for its annual Toys for Tots toy contest. The only problem was that I hadn't yet set up my shop or stocked up on wood, and the guild required six copies of each toy for entry. Working within those parameters, I came up with this marble maze game.

What makes this ball-in-maze so puzzling is that everything's hidden within the block. You might solve the puzzle several times and never completely figure it out. I don't know what the kids thought of the puzzles, but the big kids (a.k.a. other guild members) couldn't put them down.

Using a stop-block ensures that all the blocks are the same length and prevents the small cutoffs from getting sucked into the saw blade.

GET THE BALL ROLLING

This isn't a difficult project, but it has a few interesting wrinkles. For those who haven't tried a production run on a woodworking project, this is a good time to learn how cut-off and drilling jigs can help you make multiple projects in the same time it would take to make just one (I made eight in a weekend). Graphically challenged woodworkers (like me) will appreciate how easy it is to make custom images using your computer and a router template guide.

Begin by milling the maze block to size. I used walnut, but you can use any straight-grained hardwood. Because I didn't think that a ¾"-thick block riddled with ½"-diameter holes would survive in the hands of a 5-year-old, I made my block as thick as my stock would allow, ⅞" in this case. As you joint and plane your stock, be sure to make a few extra blocks, in case you make a mistake later on.

After ripping the stock to width on a table saw, cut your blocks to length. If you don't have a stop system on your table saw's miter gauge, make a combination stop-block/hold down for your miter saw using a strip of medium density fiberboard (MDF) and a toggle clamp. The

stop should be positioned so the blocks are cut to 4¾" long and the toggle clamp holds the work in place during the cut. Use the miter saw's hold-down clamp to secure the fixture to the miter saw's table.

MAKE A MOUNTAIN MOTIF

Once the blocks are done, shift your attention to routing a design on the face of the project. Although you might be able to rout it freehand, the template approach is safer and ensures that each box looks as good as the next. You can sketch your own design, find a computerized picture (which is what I did) or use the full-size template on page 28. I chose a design that had a foreground and a background, and it required two templates. Use a spray adhesive to affix the patterns to a ⅜" x 8¼" x 14½" piece of Masonite.

Because the mountain motif has a foreground and a background, you'll first decide what you want to be in front. Then use a jigsaw or scrollsaw to cut the outlines on the Masonite. Next, place the maze block on the underside of the template and glue stop-blocks around the maze block in a U shape to capture the maze block.

Use double-stick tape and the dogs on your bench to secure the maze block to the routing template.

These stop-blocks will help accurately position future blocks.

Here's how to clamp your template and work for routing: Put a maze block in place against the stop-blocks on the template. Using the dog on your bench vise and a dog in your benchtop, clamp the stop-block on the template to the maze block. You also could use some double-stick tape for additional security. You are now ready to rout your pattern.

Rout the foreground first. Use a ⅛"-diameter down-cut bit and a guide bushing as shown above. I used the bit and bushing set that came with my router inlay set (available at Woodcraft, 800-535-4486 or woodcraft.com, item #09I16, $48.99).

To ensure that you follow the template, lightly press the bushing against the Masonite at all times. Now flip the template around and repeat this process with the background, but remember to stop routing where the rear mountain intersects with the front range.

DRILL A MAZE

Now it's time to make the maze. To start, use a marking gauge to scribe a center line on one of your blocks, then carefully lay out the locations for the holes as shown in the diagram on page 28. You might also want to use a nail set to dimple the starting point of each hole to prevent the bit from wandering.

To bore the holes, use a drill press and new ½"-diameter brad-point bit. You will need to set up a fence system on your drill press and a stop to make this procedure work. It doesn't need to be complicated or expensive. Two

You'll need a full-size drill press to bore the deepest holes in the maze. The machine's throw should be at least 2 ". Make sure to clamp the block to a fence. If the box moves even a little, the bit might catch and ruin your block. (Remember the extra blocks you cut?) Use a stop-block to eliminate errors that come from repetitive measurements.

pieces of wood screwed into an L shape makes a good fence, as shown on page 27.

Because drilling into existing holes can cause the bit to wander or blow out the grain, start with the deepest holes. First drill the four 2¾"-deep holes, then the two 2½"-deep holes (one from each side), then one 2"-deep hole, four 1¼"-deep holes, then one ½"-deep hole and finally, eight ¼"-deep holes.

Drilling 20 holes per box isn't as time consuming as it might seem – if you use a stop-block and drill all the same-depth holes at once. The real trick to success is to make sure that the maze block is correctly oriented against your stop when you make each hole. (If you drill a hole on the opposite end of the block, you may create an impossible maze.)

When drilling the holes, stack all of your blocks to one side of machine so that the mountains are facing you. After each round of holes, make sure the blocks are still

When making tapered plugs, drill until the cutter starts to chamfer the top edge to be sure that you're getting the taper. Drilling through one edge of the plug stock makes it easier on the cutter and allows you to pop off plugs with a chisel.

You can make a tiny router table simply by attaching a MDF fence to your router's base. Pivot the fence into the ogee bit until the roundover section pokes through.

correctly oriented before drilling the next hole. When you're done drilling, make sure to shake out all the chips that could clog the maze. If you see any tear-out where holes intersect, wrap sandpaper around a dowel to sand the hole smooth.

PLUG IT UP

The block really isn't a maze until the outside holes are plugged. For a gap-free look, use a tapered plug cutter. It's worth noting that even though the plug will only be $1/8$" to $3/16$" thick, you'll still need to make a full-length plug, because the top of the cutter forms the taper.

After cutting the plugs from a piece of contrasting wood, pop them off with a chisel, then glue them into the maze box. When the glue has dried, trim the plugs with a backsaw, then sand or plane the edges and ends until everything is flush and smooth.

END OF THE TUNNEL

To ease the edges of the maze blocks, you can use a block plane or sandpaper, but I got the small, tight radius I wanted by using the roundover portion of an ogee bit. To do this, I made a small router fence from a scrap piece of

CUTTING LIST

No.	Item	Dimensions (inches)			Material
		T	W	L	
1	Maze block	$7/8$	$3 1/4$	$4 3/4$	Hardwood
1	Template	$3/8$	$8 1/4$	$14 1/2$	Masonite
6	Template stops	$3/4$	$3/4$	5	Scrap
18	Plugs	$1/2$ dia.			Hardwood

ADDITIONAL SUPPLIES

One $7/16$"-diameter ball bearing available from most home center stores 2 finish nails

MDF and positioned it so that only the bottom part of the bit contacted the wood.

Now you can insert the ball bearing and give your maze a test run. To keep the ball in the game, insert finish nails through the backside of the puzzle at the maze's entrance and exit.

To finish the game, sand the boxes to #220-grit, color in one of the ranges with a felt-tip marker to make it stand out, then spray on several coats of lacquer.

Face routing templates

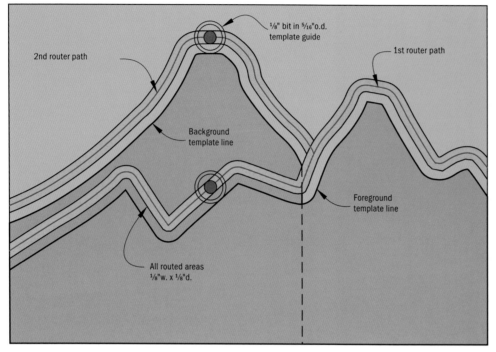

⅛" bit in ⁵/₁₆"o.d. template guide

2nd router path

1st router path

Background template line

Foreground template line

All routed areas ⅛"w. x ⅛"d.

Horizontal section

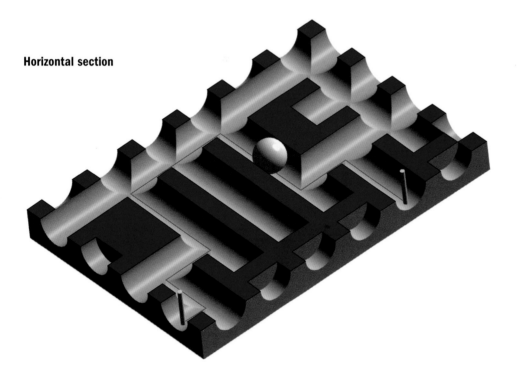

Plan

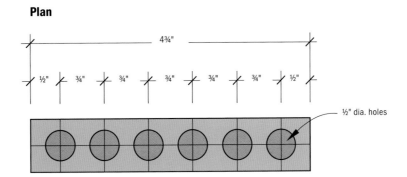

4¾"

½" ¾" ¾" ¾" ¾" ¾" ½"

½" dia. holes

Profile

½"

¾"

¾"

¾"

½"

Elevation section

½" dia. plugs

F   A   A   A   F   A

B   B

F   D

D   C

E •   F

D   F   F   F   D   F

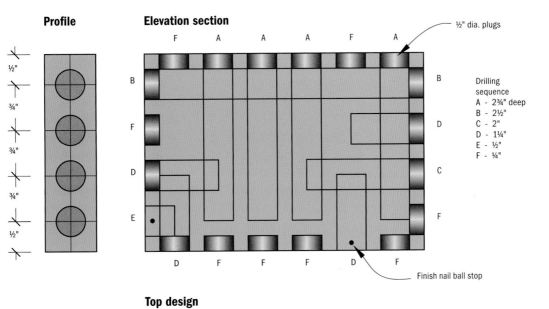

Drilling
sequence
A - 2¾" deep
B - 2½"
C - 2"
D - 1¼"
E - ½"
F - ¼"

Finish nail ball stop

Top design

3¼"

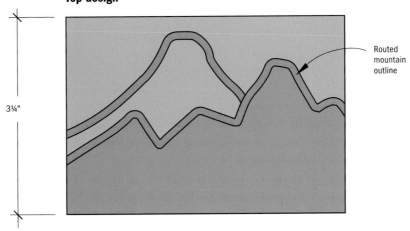

Routed
mountain
outline

GAMES

CHAPTER FIVE

GAME TABLE

by Glen D. Huey

Back in the day, gentlemen would sit for hours at the local barbershops and while away the time discussing the day's events and playing checkers. Hours might be spent sliding pieces from square to square.

Jumping the opponent's checkers was the way to clear his pieces from the board and to reach his back line where one would utter those fateful words, "king me." The king, two stacked checkers, possessed new powers that would allow it to move in new directions. With those added powers came a better chance at clearing the board.

Removing all of the opponents checkers would make one the winner. It would allow him to obtain the local title or possibly begin a heated argument that went on for days by itself.

What could be better than to bring those long passed days back into your home with the building of this game table? The time spent with family members playing at this table will bridge many gaps and start many a conversation about life.

IT ALL STARTS AT THE TOP

The table top is the most important part of this table. That's where we begin. Select the material for the frame and make a 45° cut on both ends of the pieces leaving 23" of length at the long side of each piece. Cut all four pieces the same length.

The 23" figure comes about due to the size of the game board. The board is 18" square and using the stock for the frame at 2½". To wrap the board with this stock you need to have pieces for the frame at 23". If you choose to change the board size remember to adjust the frame size as well.

With the frame pieces cut to length, you'll need to use the pocket-screw jig to locate and drill two holes per end on two of the pieces (see photo below left).

Putting the frame together is as simple as driving the pocket screws. Place a clamp on the piece that is accepting the screws so it won't move. Position the pocketed piece against the clamped frame member and drive the screws to make the connection. Repeat this step for each corner and the frame will come together.

For extra reinforcement I added screws to the corners (lower right) then cut plugs from matching stock to fill the countersink area. Add a small amount of glue to the holes and tap in the plugs.

Next, prepare the stock for the board supports. Each piece has a mitered 45° cut at each end made at the miter

CUTTING LIST

No.	Part	Stock	T x W x L (Inches)	Millimeters
4	Board frame	Oak	¾ × 2½ × 23	19 × 64 × 584
4	Board supports	Poplar	¾ × 1½ × 19½	19 × 38 × 495
1	Board	Plywood	¾ × 18 × 18	19 × 457 × 457
2	Inside fit aprons	Poplar	¾ × 3½ × 19½	19 × 89 × 495
2	Outside fit aprons	Poplar	¾ × 3½ × 21	19 × 89 × 533
4	Legs (pre-miter)	Poplar	¾ × 3½ × 27	19 × 89 × 686
2	Leg connectors	Poplar	¾ × 2½ × 6	19 × 64 × 152
2	Stretchers	Poplar	¾ × 3½ × 19½	19 × 89 × 495

Set the angled cut flat to the jig and drill the holes perpendicular to the cut end. The remaining pieces will accept the screws and no holes are required.

When driving the pocket screws, it's best to clamp whatever you can to the bench. This helps to ensure a tight, flush fit when the screw is tight.

Plan

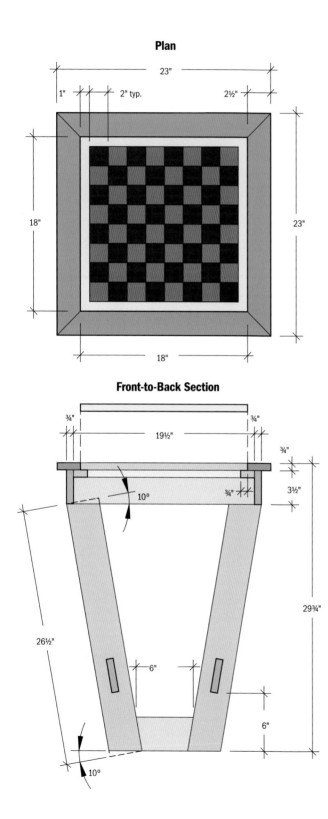

23"

1" 2" typ. 2½"

18" 23"

18"

Front-to-Back Section

¾" 19½" ¾"

¾"

10° ¾"

3½"

26½"

6"

6"

10°

29¾"

Side-to-Side Section

21"

19½"

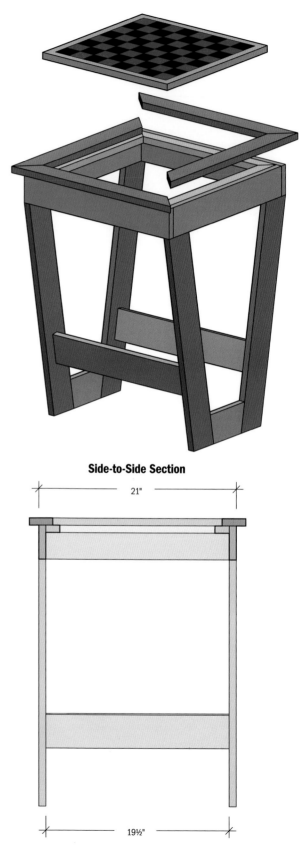

Drill a hole with a tapered countersink at each corner, four in total, then add a screw to help to hold the corners of the frame tight.

Attach the board supports using screws.

Fit the apron parts to the board supports.

Use pocket-hole screws to assemble the apron parts.

saw. These pieces are attached to the inside edge of the frame with ¾" lying on the frame and ¾" sticking into the center area to catch the game board when it is positioned. Attach the support pieces with #8 x 1¼" wood screws. Be sure to use the tapered countersink for these holes too.

A STRONG LEG TO STAND ON

The apron for the table is built to snugly fit around the support pieces. The best method to gather accurate sizes is to use the support frame to align the apron. Two pieces are the inside fit aprons. These pieces are cut to the same length as the support pieces. The two outside fit aprons will extend past the support pieces and cover the ends of

the inside fit aprons. Return to the pocket-screw jig to cut two holes per end on the inside fit apron pieces.

With the holes cut, connect the apron pieces with the pocket screws. The assembled apron should just slip over the support pieces and allow the top to fit into the apron. Don't make the connection of the top to the apron just yet. You'll want to separate the two assemblies before you are finished with construction.

The legs are started at the miter saw. Set the saw for an 80° cut or 10° off of a square cut of 90°. Position the material for two legs at the saw and cut the angle at what is to be the top of each leg. Leave the saw set at that angle for the next set of cuts on the legs.

Using a miter saw, cut a 10° miter on both ends of each leg. These cuts should be parallel.

After cutting the leg connectors to length, attach them to the legs. Make two of these leg assemblies.

Attach each leg assembly to the bottom of the apron assembly using pocket screws.

Lay out the location for the stretchers and attach them to the legs.

Set the top apron assembly on one side and position the angled cut on a leg against the bottom edge of the aprons. Pull a measuring tape from the bottom edge of the apron and mark at 25½" down the leg. This is where the second cut of the leg goes.

Making that second cut is a snap. Position the leg material so that both legs are flush at the top end and cradled into the saw tight to the fence. Slide the two pieces, making sure that they stay aligned, into position to make another angled cut at the mark (upper left photo). It is important to have the cuts angled the correct way. When this cut is complete you'll have a parallelogram shape to

the legs or both cuts angle in the same direction. Repeat the steps for the second set of legs.

Next, add pocket-screw holes to the top end of each leg and align them with the bottom edge of the apron making sure that the edge of the leg lines up with the side of the apron. It doesn't really matter which opposing aprons you select to attach the legs to since the apron is square, but I attached the legs so the end grain of the outside aprons sat on the leg top – there may be additional support with this choice.

Add the legs to one side of the table, then cut the leg connector to fit in position. This connector also cuts at the same angle as the legs. Make the cut on one end then flip

Measure and mark the game board itself, using the table frame as your guide.

To lay out the checker grid itself, start from the center and measure out. It's much easier.

After taping off the 1" border, a base coat of black paint is applied to the whole board.

Stick tape down first in one direction, skipping every other space. Repeat this pattern in the other direction, then trim the tape and remove where doubled.

Apply two coats of red paint over all the exposed squares. Again alternate directions between coats to hide brush strokes.

With the paint dry, remove the tape to reveal the checkerboard pattern. I retaped the board to add a third contrasting color to the bare wood border.

the piece, measure the distance between the legs at a mark that is 2½" above the floor and make the second cut at that point. In this scenario you'll have the cuts set at opposing angles. Place two pocket-screw holes at each end and attach the connector to the legs. Repeat the process for the second leg assembly and you're ready for the stretchers.

The stretchers have square cut ends and pocket holes, two at each end, that allow you to attach them to the legs. Position the stretchers to the legs with the screw holes facing inside the table. I like these stretchers to be centered in the leg. To accomplish this easily I cut a scrap at the miter saw to the appropriate width, 1⅜" for this example, placed it at the front edge of the leg, pulled the stretchers tight to the back of the scrap and set the screws to make the connection. The base is complete.

MAKING THE GAME BOARD

Cut and fit the piece of plywood that is the game board to the opening in the table. This piece should be a loose fit so it can be removed if necessary. You see, you can also have a different game on the bottom of the board.

To mill this board use your jigsaw to cut close to the layout lines and then handplane to bring everything into shape. Remember that if you're cutting across the grain of the plywood it is best to score a line with a sharp utility knife before cutting. That way as you cut to the line the top veneer of the plywood will not splinter.

Once the game board is fit you are ready to complete the table. Add the plugs to the top frame if you haven't already, install pocket-hole fillers into any hole that is easily visible and sand everything to #150 grit. Use #100-grit sandpaper to knock off any sharp edges and move to the finishing stage.

The game board is a checker board and to make your own board you need a few additional tools. Gather a utility knife, framing square (or square of some kind) and a roll of painter's tape that is 2" wide. Of course you'll need two or three different colors of acrylic latex paint.

To complete the table I applied a couple of coats of black paint to the base, then added a top coat to protect the paint from scuffing. Finally, I added a coat of Watco oil to the top/frame of the table.

To begin the board you'll need to layout the lines that define the checker squares. Find the center of the board and draw a line across the entire piece. Next, move each way in 2" increments each time, drawing a line as before. You should end up with eight squares and 1" of space on either edge which will be the outside border of the board.

Rotate the board 90° and repeat these steps for the opposing lines. Make sure that you continue the lines clear to the edge of the plywood piece. These will become important after the first layer of paint. You now have the 64 spaces for the checkerboard.

PAINT MAKES THE SQUARE

Add painter's tape to the outside edges of the squares to protect the borders from the first paint color. Traditionally, black and red are the colors of the checkerboard, but there is no reason you couldn't choose different colors. I selected black for the first layer. Whatever color you decide upon, make the first layer the darker of the two.

Apply the paint in a light coat moving from side to side on the board. When that coat is dry (you can speed it along with a hair dryer), add a second coat of the same color, brushing in the perpendicular direction. This coat completes the first layer of paint.

Remove the tape from the borders. See those lines for the layout? Stretch the tape from end to end aligning it with the lines. Apply tape to every other section as shown. Rotate the board and add tape in the second direction as well.

Now you need to remove the tape from any areas where the tape is double layered. Align the rule or straightedge to the tape and use a utility knife to cut the tape on all four sides of each square that needs to be removed. Carefully peel away the tape to expose the black painted surface below. Each square will have two thicknesses of tape.

Once the necessary areas are removed it is time to add paint. For this layer you need the second color, and two coats will be needed to cover the exposed areas. Begin by brushing on one coat moving from top to bottom. The second coat will be applied moving from side to side. This process provides better coverage. After the second layer is dry, you can peel all remaining tape to expose the painted checkerboard.

To complete the painting you will need to apply tape around the outer edge of the checkerboard. The tape will be the barrier that will prohibit paint from touching the completed squares. I elected to paint a third color – one that will show favorably against the oak of the frame. You can also decide to allow the border to match the second color added to the checkerboard.

The completed board fits into the frame of the top. All that's left to complete the project is to apply paint to the base. I used black and added a layer of an oil/varnish finish for protection. Apply two coats of Watco's Special Walnut finish to the oak.

Set this game table in your home and rekindle the past with a rousing game of checkers. Will you be kinged and become the local champion or will you succumb to another master of the house?

CHAPTER SIX

KUBB

by Tom Caspar

If you enjoy picnics by playing a relaxing lawn game with the family, you're going to love Kubb. What, you've never heard of it? Legend has it that the Vikings played it, but whether that's true or not, Kubb is certainly gaining popularity – Kubb tournaments are now played all over the world.

All you need to play Kubb (pronounced Koob) is an open, flat area about 15' by 25', two people (although teams are more fun), and a set of Kubb pieces.

While the rules aren't very complicated, I'm going to pass on explaining the details here and direct you to a website (usakubb.org/rules). Basically, the idea is to knock over small squat blocks (called kubbs) by throwing sticks at them – underhand. (The sticks are called batons.) The kubbs are lined up on opposite sides of the playing field, which is defined by four stakes.

Each team stands on opposite sides of the field. The first side to knock over all of their kubbs must then knock over the King, which stands in the center of the field. There's definitely a strategy involved, which is why the game is sometimes called Viking Chess.

THE WOOD

You can use just about any kind of wood to make a set of Kubb pieces. Usually, all of the pieces are made from the same species of wood and are the same color. I made this set from two different species – one for each team – just for fun.

The king is 3½" square, so some folks make their set from 4x4 construction lumber. While that avoids having to glue up thinner stock, this wood is prone to splintering when it gets knocked about, so it's not ideal. Commercial sets are usually made from yellow poplar. It's relatively inexpensive and won't splinter, but it's bland in appearance.

I made this set from 8/4 (2" thick) walnut and ash. That's just the right thickness to make the batons, which are 1¾" dia. The king and kubbs are composed of two pieces glued together.

MAKING THE SET

The kubb pieces are just simple blocks (see the Cutting List, page 42). Mill four pieces 1⁷/₁₆" thick, 3" wide and 32" long. Glue them together to make two blanks, then mill the blanks on all sides, making them 2¾" square. Cut the blanks into five kubbs apiece. Soften all of the kubbs' edges with a router, using a ⅛" roundover bit.

Turn the batons on the lathe. If you don't have a lathe, make them octagonal. The stakes can be round or octagonal. I also made an optional mallet for pounding in the stakes.

The king could simply be a plain block, like the kubbs, but here's how I made a two-part king with a crown. Mill

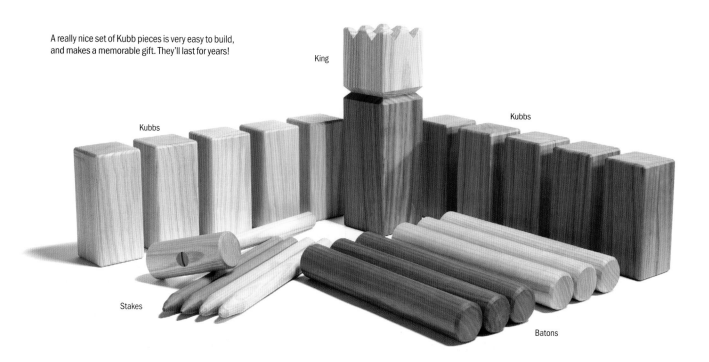

A really nice set of Kubb pieces is very easy to build, and makes a memorable gift. They'll last for years!

King

Kubbs

Kubbs

Stakes

Batons

1

Begin making the King by beveling the end of a large walnut block. Make the same cuts on a shorter block of ash.

2

Use a jig, made on a drill press, to drill dowel holes in the end of the walnut block. Turn over the jig to drill mating holes in the ash block.

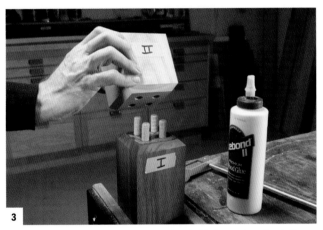

3

Glue the pieces together. The numbers marked on the blocks correspond to similar numbers on the drilling jig. These marks ensure that the holes will align.

4

Saw V-shaped notches to make the King's crown. Rotate the King after each cut. Make these cuts in small stages to avoid trapping offcuts and cutting too deep.

two pieces of walnut and two pieces of ash 1^{13}/$_{16}$" thick, 3¾" wide and 10" long. Glue them together and mill them into 3½" square blocks. Cut the blocks to final length (the ash block is extra-long so it's safe to joint and plane.) Bevel one end of both blocks (**Photo 1** and **Fig. A**). Stand the ash block on the walnut block and decide which faces should be on the same side. Mark two mating faces I and II.

Join the two blocks with ⅜" or ½" dowels, using a jig for drilling the holes (**Photo 2**). This jig is reversible: drilling from opposite sides of the jig ensures that the holes in both blocks will be aligned. The main part of the jig should be at least 1" thick. You could cut this piece from the leftover ash block or make a new one; in any case, it must be exactly the same size as the walnut and ash blocks. Drill four holes through the piece using a drill

press to ensure that the holes are perpendicular. Nail or glue four small pieces of wood around the jig.

Before drilling the holes, mark the jig. Place the jig on the walnut block, then place the ash block in the jig. Mark I and II on one of the outer pieces of the jig, corresponding to the marks on the blocks, as shown in the photo. Remove the ash block. Clamp the jig to the walnut block and drill four holes. Remove the jig, turn it over and clamp it to the ash block. Drill the mating holes. Glue dowels in the holes and glue the blocks together (**Photo 3**).

To make the king's crown, lay out the V cuts on just one of the king's faces (**Fig. A**). The sawing process is very easy, but you have to be careful (**Photo 4**). Basically, you just need to make two cuts (Cut 1 and Cut 2) rotating the block four times for each cut. However, to avoid kickback, you can't make any small offcuts that will get trapped under the king. Instead of cutting right on the line, start each cut ⅛" off the center of the V and raise the saw blade up only ³/₁₆". Rotate the king and make 3 more of the same cuts. Then adjust the king's position so the saw cuts ⅛" closer to the V line. Raise the blade about ⅜" high and saw again. Move the King one more time and adjust the blade's height until you're cutting exactly on the line. Don't cut right to the bottom of the V, though – clean this waste out later with a chisel. When you're done, ease all the edges with the roundover bit, including the top of the crown.

Toss all the pieces in a small duffel bag, pack the picnic basket and go have fun!

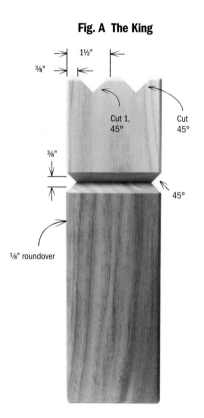

Fig. A The King

1½"

⅜"

Cut 1, 45°

Cut 45°

⅜"

45°

⅛" roundover

CUTTING LIST

Qty.	Part	Dimensions (TxWxL)
1	King	3½" x 3½" x 11¾" (a)
10	Kubb	2¾" x 2¾" x 6"
6	Baton	1¾" dia. x 11¾"
4	Stake	1" dia. x 11¾"

Notes:

a) For a two-part king, the top is 3¾" long; the bottom is 8" long.

CHAPTER SEVEN
TABLE HOCKEY

by Randy Johnson

Figure A Exploded View

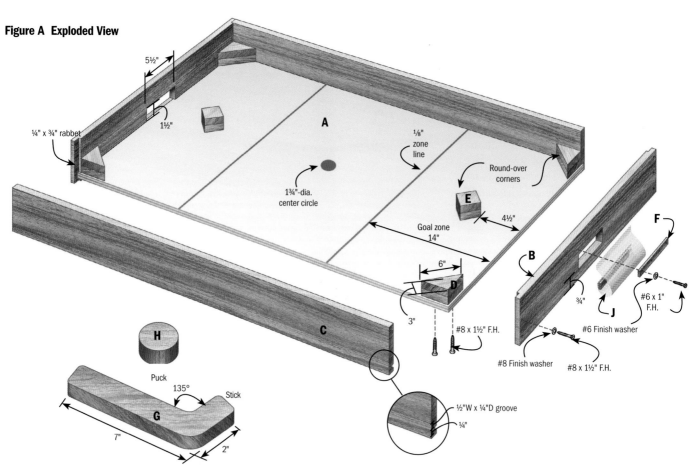

Cutting List Overall Dimensions: 4¼"T x 32"W x 48"L

CUTTING LIST

PART	NAME	QTY.	DIMENSIONS (T W L)	MATERIAL	NOTES
A	Bottom	1	½" x 31" x 47"	Birch plywood	
B	Ends	2	¾" x 4¼" x 32"	Oak	
C	Sides	2	¾" x 4¼" x 47"	Oak	
D	Corner blocks	4	1½" x 3" x 6"	Oak	Cut from two pieces of ¾" x 3½" x 24" lumber glued together.
E	Goalie blocks	2	1½" x 2" x 2"	Oak	Cut from two pieces of ¾" x 2½" x 18" lumber glued together.
F	Net boards	4	¼" x ¾" x 7½"	Oak	
G	Sticks	2	½" x 2" x 7"	Oak or birch plywood	
H	Pucks	2	½"T x 1¾" dia.	Oak or birch plywood	
J	Nets	2	7½"H x 7½"W	Mesh fabric	

PROJECT REQUIREMENTS AT A GLANCE

POWER TOOLS	MATERIALS		TOTAL COST:
Table saw	½ in. birch plywood	Netting	About $75
Dado blade	¾ in. oak lumber	Screws	
Jigsaw	Stain	Finish washers	
Drill	Paint		
Sander	Varnish		

L ooking for a great holiday gift project? This table hockey game is a blast to play, even for adults, and it's so simple, you can make it even if your gift-building time is running short. It's made from easy-to-get materials, and the finish is all water-based, so it goes on quickly.

It's basically a shallow box, made from ¾" hardwood (I used oak) with a playing surface of ½" birch plywood. Add some small pieces of mesh fabric (available from a fabric store) for the goals, a couple of strategically placed goalie blocks, a pair of sticks and a puck, and you're ready to play!

HOW TO BUILD IT

1. Mill the end and side boards (B, C) to final size and cut the grooves for the bottom panel (A, **Fig. A**, page 44).
2. Cut the rabbets in the end boards (**Photo 1**). Use an auxiliary wood fence so you can run your dado blade right next to it. This setup also allows the auxiliary fence to serve as a guide when you cut the rabbets.

1

Cut rabbets in the end boards, so the corners are strong enough to take abuse. Use an auxiliary fence to protect the main fence from damage. A ½" groove at the bottom edge houses the plywood playing surface.

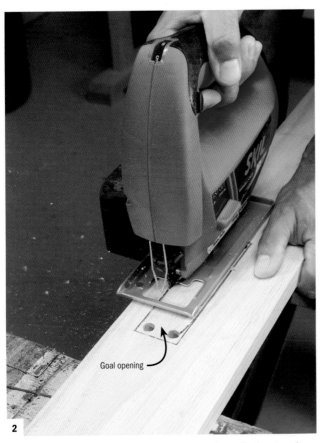

2

Saw goal openings with a jigsaw. Holes near each corner make starting the cuts and turning the corners easy. Smooth the inside of the goal opening with a file or sanding block.

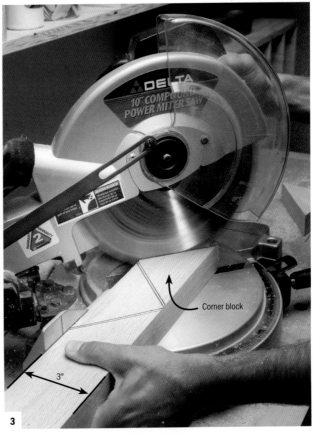

3

Cut the corner blocks from glued up ¾" boards. These blocks keep the puck from getting trapped in the corners and allow interesting bank shots.

4

Finish all the parts before you assemble them. After the blue stain on the bottom panel is dry, tape off and paint the zone lines and the center circle.

3. Cut out the opening for the goals using a jigsaw or scrollsaw (**Photo 2**).
4. Glue and clamp together two layers of ¾" lumber for the corner blocks (D). Wipe off any glue that squeezes out. When the glue is dry, rip the board to 3" wide for the corner blocks. Make the goalie blocks (E) the same way.
5. Cut the corner blocks and goalie blocks to final size (**Photo 3**) using your miter saw or table saw. You'll notice that the glued up lumber stock is much longer than actually needed. This extra length gives you more to hold for safer mitering and crosscutting. Cut the net boards (F).
6. Use your band saw or scrollsaw to saw the sticks (G) and pucks (H) from either oak lumber or birch ply-

Finish washer

5

Assemble the parts with flat head screws and finish washers. Finish washers provide extra bearing surface for the screw heads and don't require countersinking.

Double sided tape

6

Attach the goal netting with the net boards and screws. Leave the net open on the sides to make it easy to retrieve the puck. You're ready to play!

wood. Make a couple extra pucks, so you won't have to take a time-out if a puck flies off the table and rolls under the couch.

7. Sand and finish all the parts. I used water-based stain, paint and finish. Water-based finishes tend to raise the grain after they are applied, which makes a rough finish. To prevent this, raise the grain first with a moist sponge. After the wood dries, do your final sanding. Then apply the stain to all the parts. When the blue stain on the bottom panel is dry, tape off and paint the zone lines and center circle (**Photo 4**). Finally, brush on the clear topcoat finish.

8. Assemble the hockey table with screws and finish washers (**Photo 5**). Drill shank and pilot holes in the sides to prevent splitting the wood or stripping the screw heads.

9. Attach the netting (J) over the goal openings with the net boards (F). The bottom net board goes inside the net and the top net board goes outside the net (**Photo 6**). Hold the netting in place with a bit of double-sided tape during assembly. You can substitute almost any kind of fabric for the netting, if you wish.

10. Attach corner and goalie blocks (D, E) with screws from the bottom.

It's game time! Go for the goal!

Table Hockey Rules

You can play table hockey two ways. The first is free play. Players start with the puck on the center circle and both hit it around until a goal is scored. The only limit is that a player may not play the puck within the goal zone of the other player. If the puck flies off the table during play, return it to the center circle and resume playing.

The second way to play is to take turns. Each player takes a predetermined number of shots. Two swings per player is common, but the exact number is up to you. You can handicap a better player by giving him or her fewer swings than a less experienced player. The entire rink area is open for play. If a puck is knocked off the table, it's turned over to the other player, who then gets to take one additional shot during his or her turn. Of course, it's also fun to make up your own rules!

CHAPTER EIGHT
TABLETOP FOOSBALL

by A.J. Hamler

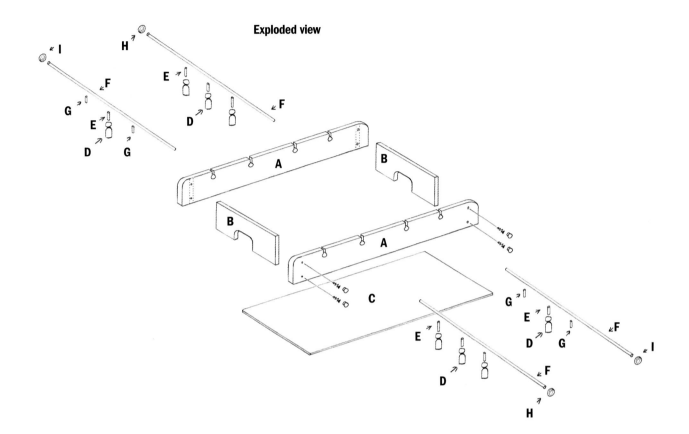

Exploded view

CUTTING LIST

Overall dimensions: 11½" wide x 24" long x 3¾" high

Ref	Qty.	Part	Stock	Dimensions (T, W, L)		
A	2	Long sides	Pine	¾"	3½"	24" (a)
B	2	Goal sides	Pine	¾"	3½"	10" (a)
C	1	Bottom	Plywood	¼"	11-½"	24"
D	8	Players	Hardwood doll	⅝"	n/a	1⅝" (b)
E	8	Player mounts	Hardwood dowel	¼"	n/a	1¼"
F	4	Control rods	Hardwood dowel	½"	n/a	20"
G	4	Goalie rod stops	Hardwood dowel	¼"	n/a	1"
H	2	Kicker rod knobs	Hardwood ball	1"	n/a	n/a
I	2	Goalie rod knobs	Hardwood ball	1¼"	n/a	n/a
J	1	Playing ball	Hardwood ball	1"	n/a	n/a

NOTES

(a) Parts A and B can be cut from standard 1x4 pine, which actually measures ¾" thick by 3½" wide.

(b) Usually sold as "Wooden Doll" or "Wooden People" or something similar.

ADDITIONAL MATERIALS

Hardwood button plugs (8 needed)

F oosball simulates the field game of soccer, and dedicated foosball tables have been a staple of rec rooms and arcades for decades. Full-size tables vary, but most are around 48" long and feature four control rods and 11 little players per side. However, with a downsized game board and fewer players, foosball is easily adaptable to a tabletop version. For this project we'll cut the game board to about half size, decrease the number of controls to two per side, and the number of little players to four per team. Your kids will still have plenty of play action, and when they're done the game is easy to store in a closet or under a bed.

BUILDING THE TABLETOP FOOSBALL

The game board is a basic rectangular box with 3½" high sides, so you can cut all four sides of the game box to length from standard 1x4 pine, which is already 3½" wide. A miter box is your best bet for cutting these squarely. Transfer the Goal Pattern from page 50 to the center of the two shorter pieces, and cut the opening with a coping saw, jigsaw or scrollsaw (**Photo 1**).

Prepare the game box long sides by first rounding off the top corners with a jigsaw or coping saw, per the Side End Detail drawing on page 50. Now, lay out the locations of the side holes that will accept the control rods. Measure

Side End Detail

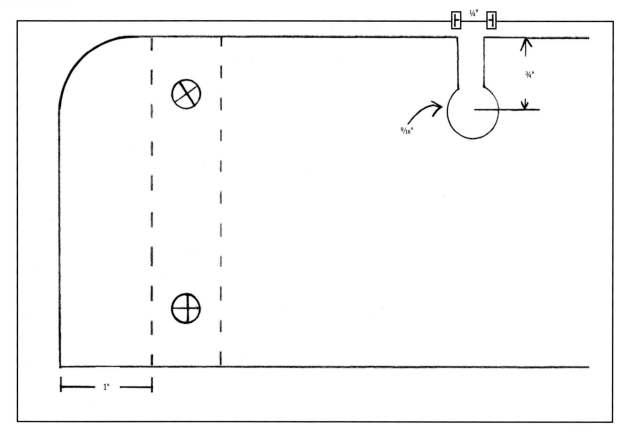

Goal Pattern

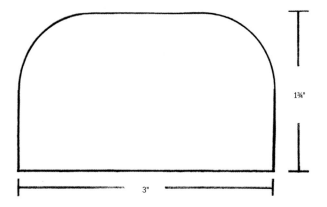

and mark at 4½", 9½", 14½" and 19½"; each of these marks should be exactly ¾" from the top edge. With the marks laid out, clamp the sides, atop a piece of scrap, to your bench or worktable, and drill ⁹/₁₆" holes on your marks as shown in **Photo 2**. Since the control rods are ½", a ⁹/₁₆" hole will allow them to move freely without binding.

These side holes are slotted on the top in an inverted keyhole shape to accommodate the mounting dowels of the little players when inserting the rods for play. Mark a ¼" wide slot directly above and centered over each of the holes, then cut the waste free. In **Photo 3** I'm using a coping saw, which is really the fastest way to go, but you can also cut these with a jigsaw or scrollsaw if you like. Since the player mounting dowels are ¼", cut these slots directly on the line, which will create a slot just a tad wider than ¼". With the ⁹/₁₆" hole drilled at ¾" from the top edge, the length of this slot will be a bit shorter than ½". You can see these slotted holes in the Side End Detail drawing.

Fold a piece of #100-grit sandpaper and sand the interior and edges of the slots smooth, rounding edges slightly,

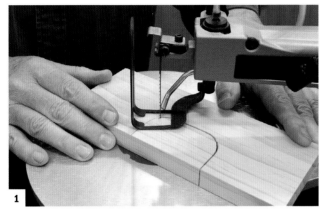

1

Cut out the goal opening with a coping saw or, as here, a scrollsaw.

2

Measure and mark carefully, then drill the rod holes at the top of the game side pieces.

3

Create a keyhole by cutting down to the rod hole with a coping saw.

4

Apply glue to the ends of the goal sides and clamp the assembly until dry.

then give the entire side a good sanding as well. Repeat with #150-grit paper.

Mark perpendicular lines 1" from each end across the inside faces of the long sides. Assemble the game box by applying glue to the ends of the short goal sides and clamping them on your lines between the two long sides, then check the assembly for square, as in **Photo 4**. Insetting the two goal ends gives a playing field measuring 20½" long.

When dry, unclamp the assembly and countersink pilot holes for two 1⁵⁄₈" screws at each corner to reinforce the joints (**Photo 5**). Drill the countersinks deeply enough so that once the screws are driven in, there's a ³⁄₁₆" to ¼" space above the screw heads. This will give us room to install wooden button plugs to hide the screws.

A jigsaw works best to cut the game box bottom to size. To get a perfectly straight cut, temporarily clamp a strip of wood to the workpiece offset the width of the jigsaw base, as in **Photo 6**.

Flip the game box upside down and apply glue all around the top edges. Put the bottom into place, aligning

the edges all around, and attach the bottom permanently by driving ¾" or 1" brads in through the bottom. Note in **Photo 7** that I've penciled a nailing guide showing the center of the box sides all the way around. Be sure to set the nails just below the surface with a nail set so they can't scratch the tabletop while playing. With the bottom attached, give the plywood a light sanding if needed.

Let's go back to those screws in the box assembly and make them disappear. Apply just a dab of glue around the inside of the countersink and tap in wood button plugs, which will cover the screw heads and add a nice detail to the sides of the game box (**Photo 8**).

The game box is now complete, so set it aside as we shift attention to the players and control rods. The players are small wooden doll bodies available at any craft store or large fabric store with a craft section. These are fairly standard, but for reference the ones I got were ⁵⁄₈" in diameter by 1⁵⁄₈" in length.

The players attach to the control rods by way of short ¼"-diameter dowels, so drill the top of each player using a ¼" drill bit to a depth of ³⁄₈". To make this task easier,

5

Reinforce the assembly by countersinking pilot holes and driving in 1⅝" screws.

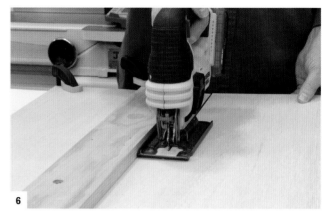

6

Cut the box bottom with a jigsaw. A clamped-on guide ensures a straight cut.

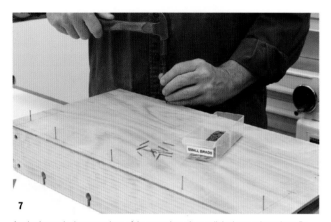

7

Apply glue to the bottom edges of the game box, then nail the bottom into place. Be sure to set the nails just below the surface.

8

Put just a dab of glue around the edges of the countersinks, then tap in wooden button plugs.

create a quick jig to hold the little players for drilling – it'd be nearly impossible to drill them safely otherwise. Drill a few ⅝" holes in a line down the center of a small piece of scrap. Now, use a scrollsaw, jigsaw or coping saw to cut the scrap in two right through the holes, creating two halves with partial holes. Place the wooden players in these half-holes, add the other side of the scrap and clamp the two sides together. This forms an assembly that you can now clamp to your workbench for drilling, as shown in **Photo 9**. I've used masking tape to ensure I don't drill any deeper than ⅜". Depending on how many holes you made in your jig, you'll need to do this a few times to drill all eight of the wooden players.

While you still have the ¼" bit in your drill, move on to the control rods and mark the hole locations. For the center kicker control rods, mark for the three wooden players at 5½", 8½" and 11½". There's only one player on the goalie rods, right in the center. However, these rods

need a couple of stops to control how far the rod will move. The kicker rods don't need these because the outer two players act as stops. Mark the goalie rod at 6", 8½" and 11". Note that the two outermost holes are a bit farther in than on the kicker rod, meaning the goalie has a wider range of movement to protect the goal.

Before drilling the rods, clamp them securely to a bench; if you have a vise, partially open it and set the rods there and clamp from the top. Drill on your marks to ⅜" deep (**Photo 10**).

Cut eight pieces of ¼" dowel to a length of 1¼" for the player mounts, and four more to 1" for the goalie stops. In **Photo 11**, you can see how to make this easy. Clamp a small block of scrap to the bed of your miter gauge so it snugly holds a length of dowel in place. Pencil in a mark to indicate the desired length to the side of the cutting slot. Slide the dowel until it touches your mark and cut, then slide and cut again until you have as many as you need.

9 Secure the wooden players in the drilling jig, then drill a ¼" hole into the center of the tops.

10 Clamp the control rod dowels onto a partially opened vise for drilling the player mounting holes.

11 A pencil mark on your miter gauge makes it easy to cut several dowels the same length.

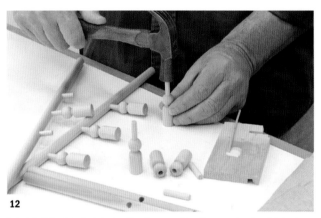

12 Put a bit of glue into the hole atop the players, and tap the mounting dowels into place.

With ⅜"-deep holes in both the wooden players and the control rods, mounting the players with the 1¼" dowels will leave ½" of open dowel between them, which will allow the rods to be inserted into the game box's slot holes. Because drilling precise hole depths can be difficult, be sure to dry-fit the players on the rods and check the distance of open dowel – if it's ½" you're golden; if it's not, shorten the mounting dowels or cut longer ones to get the length right.

Dab a very small amount of glue into the top of all eight wooden players and tap the 1¼" mounting dowels in until they seat firmly, as in **Photo 12**. Now, dab a bit of glue into the player holes in the control rods and tap the players into place. Remember that there are three players on the two center rods, but only one on the goalie rods. With the goalies in place, glue in the 1" dowel stops on either side of the goalie. You can see two completed control rods on the left in **Photo 12**.

The rods are complete and ready for use, but you can add a nice touch by gluing some knobs on the ends for surer control and an attractive detail. You can find wooden balls already drilled with ½" holes at most craft stores. If they're not drilled, you can drill your own with the same type of jig used earlier to drill the tops of the wooden players. I used 1" knobs for the two center kicker rods. For the goalie rods I wanted a better grip and so glued on slightly larger 1¼" knobs. You can use either size, or make all the knobs the same if you like.

The last step is to give the entire game a nice finish. Polyurethane varnish is perfect for this, as it not only brings out the grain and deepens the color of the wood, but it also adds a good bit of protection from rough play.

Insert the rods by turning them so the players face upward, and slide them into the slot holes. Once all the way in, swinging the players down into playing position locks the rods in the game box.

CHAPTER NINE
BOCCE

by Alan Lacer

Freehand turning of a near perfect wooden sphere without flat spots or bumps is a wonderful challenge for a turner. Whether it's for croquet, furniture drawer knobs or simply as a decorative object, the wooden sphere is a wonderful exercise in developing a form, tool control and understanding grain direction.

This project is to make wooden balls for the ancient game of bocce ball. Originating in the Middle East some 7,000 years ago, the game was popular with ancient Greeks and Romans. It hit its heyday in 16th-century Italy, where it was something of a national sport. Much of the vocabulary and manner of play stems from this period.

BOCCE BALL ESSENTIALS

To play the game you have to make either five or nine wooden balls in two sizes. One ball, the pallino or target ball, should be approximately 2¼" in diameter, in a contrasting or colored wood. The other balls, or bocce that are tossed, should be approx. 4" in diameter. Create either a full set with eight bocce or a half set of four, with one-half of each set in distinctive colors or patterns to identify two teams. Within each team you may want to create a crisscross or other pattern to distinguish individual bocce balls.

WOOD TO TURN

Turn the bocce balls and pallino from a dense hardwood such as hard maple, birch or white oak in either solid or laminated stock. If you laminate, choose glue that is water-resistant and doesn't creep at the seams, such as plastic resin or polyurethane.

SHOP-MADE CHUCKS

You have to make three different concave holding chucks to turn these balls. For the headstock side you need two different sizes that fit into your scroll chuck or a recess in a scrap block on your 3" faceplate (a "jam chuck," see **Photo 2**). On the tailstock side, make a chuck that slips over your live center (two styles are shown as examples). This tailstock chuck works for both size balls.

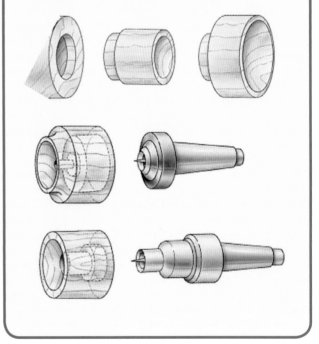

THE RULES OF BOCCE BALL

Official bocce ball is played on a court of fixed dimensions, often with walls and backstops. What most of us play is an informal version or lawn bowling. Here are the basic rules:

- There are two teams, played with two, four or eight players. In games of two or four players, you can get by with only four bocce balls. The game is a bit more interesting, though, if you play with a full set of eight balls.
- By a flip of a coin or some other means, choose one side to roll the small ball (pallino) out into the playing area. All throws must be made behind a real or imaginary foul line.
- The side that placed the pallino rolls one bocce ball as close to the pallino as possible (even touching it). This becomes the point ball.

- The opposing side rolls all of its bocce balls to see if it can come closer to the pallino than the "point ball."
- The starting team rolls the remainder of its bocce balls to see if can come closer to the pallino than any of their opponents' balls.
- Points are awarded after all bocce balls have been thrown. A point is awarded for each ball closer than any of the opponents' to the pallino. Games are played to 12, 16 or 21. Often the winner must win by at least two points.
- Yes, you may hit the pallino, your own team's previously thrown bocce or the bocce of the opposing team!

For more information, go to www.bocceballrules.net

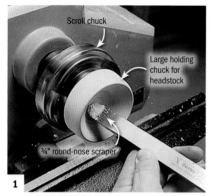

1

Begin by turning a chuck to hold the balls as they are turned. This one is for the larger balls and is held at the headstock. Work from the center out with your round-nose scraper to produce a smooth surface. Make a smaller chuck for the headstock to hold the pallino.

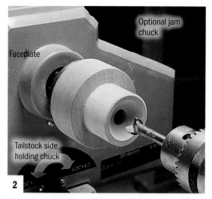

2

Turn another holding chuck for the tailstock. It needs to fit over a live center so it can spin freely. Drill or turn out the center of the chuck to match the outside diameter of the live center. Each live center requires a slightly different design. The chuck must be centered and fit snugly.

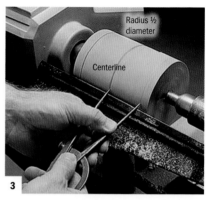

3

Lay out the size of the ball with dividers or a compass after roughing out the blank to a cylinder. Mark the centerline (red) and two radius lines (blue) that are equal to half the diameter of the cylinder. After marking, reduce the waste outside of the radius lines to approx. 1" in dia.

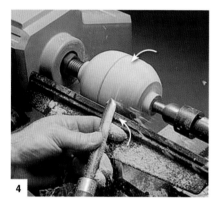

4

Rough cut the cylinder to a very crude ball form using a ½" detail gouge. Don't be too zealous in trying to hit the perfect sphere at this point—it is far too easy to cut below the curves of the final sphere. Allow considerable waste material to be trimmed away in the next step.

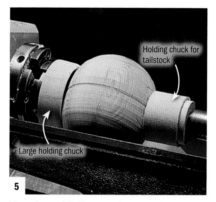

5

Mount the rough ball between the two holding chucks with the red centerline turned 90° so it's parallel to the bed or axis of the lathe. Rotate the lathe by hand a few times to be sure both sides of the red line are in alignment. When all seems right, firmly secure the block by tightening the tailstock.

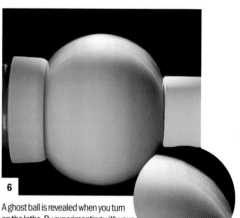

6

A ghost ball is revealed when you turn on the lathe. By experimenting with your shop lamp and different angles of viewing, you should see a definite ball with a ghost-like appearance inside the spinning blank. With light-colored woods, a dark background often helps to make the ghost more visible. Keep your lathe in the slower speed ranges (400 to 600 rpm).

HERE'S WHAT YOU NEED

- Hard maple, 4x4 by 1" (makes four bocce balls; buy twice this amount for a full set of 8). Each ball blank should be 4½" long.
- Hardwood, 2¼" by 2¼" by 2¾" (for one pallino).
- Basswood (or poplar) 3" by 3" by 2" in length (headstock side holding chuck for larger ball); two pieces 2" by 2" by 2" (headstock side holding chuck for smaller ball and for tailstock-side holding chuck that fits over the live center).
- ½" detailing gouge ground to a fingernail shape, roughing gouge, parting tool, ½" to 1" round-nose scraper, ½" or larger skew chisel.

- Outside calipers with a minimum capacity of 4½"
- Dividers or compass.
- Either a scroll chuck or a 3" faceplate with 1½"-thick piece of face-grain poplar or soft maple.
- Live center for tailstock, spur center for headstock.
- Jacobs chuck and appropriate bit for fitting tailstock-side chuck to your live center.
- Acrylic paint in two colors and a small, stiff brush.
- Wood dye.

7

Turn down to the ghost ball, using a ½" detailing gouge with a fingernail shape. Work from smaller to larger diameters on both sides of the centerline (the ball now has the same grain orientation as a face-grain bowl). Go slowly and gently, with a mixture of cutting and light scraping actions to remove waste surrounding the ghost ball.

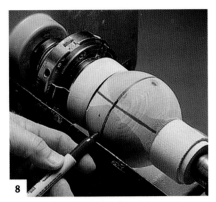

8

Draw a new centerline (the blue line) when you're finished turning.

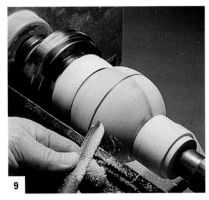

9

Continue turning with the blue line positioned parallel to the lathe's axis. The grain is again as we started (indicated by the red line), so work from larger to smaller diameter in order to work with the grain. Gently turn away the waste that was held in the holding chucks. Again, use the ghost ball as a guide.

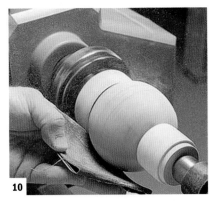

10

Sand to further refine the shape and remove minor imperfections. Randomly reposition the ball five or six times, sanding lightly between each change of position.

11

Cut narrow grooves on the larger balls with the long point (toe) of the skew chisel. Create a crisscross pattern by changing the axis of the ball. With the lathe spinning, color the grooves with unthinned acrylic paint applied with a stiff brush. Light sanding removes excess paint. The single pallino (smaller ball) is usually not grooved and can be dyed a bright color for high visibility.

SOURCES

Constantines
constantines.com
(954) 561-1716
Hard maple 4 x 4 x 18" (makes 4 bocce balls), $35.25, hard maple 2½"
square 12" long for the pallino, $7.95

Woodcraft Supply
www.woodcraft.com
(800) 225-1153
yellow powdered dye for the pallino #123837 $11.49, plus shipping.

TOYS & GADGETS

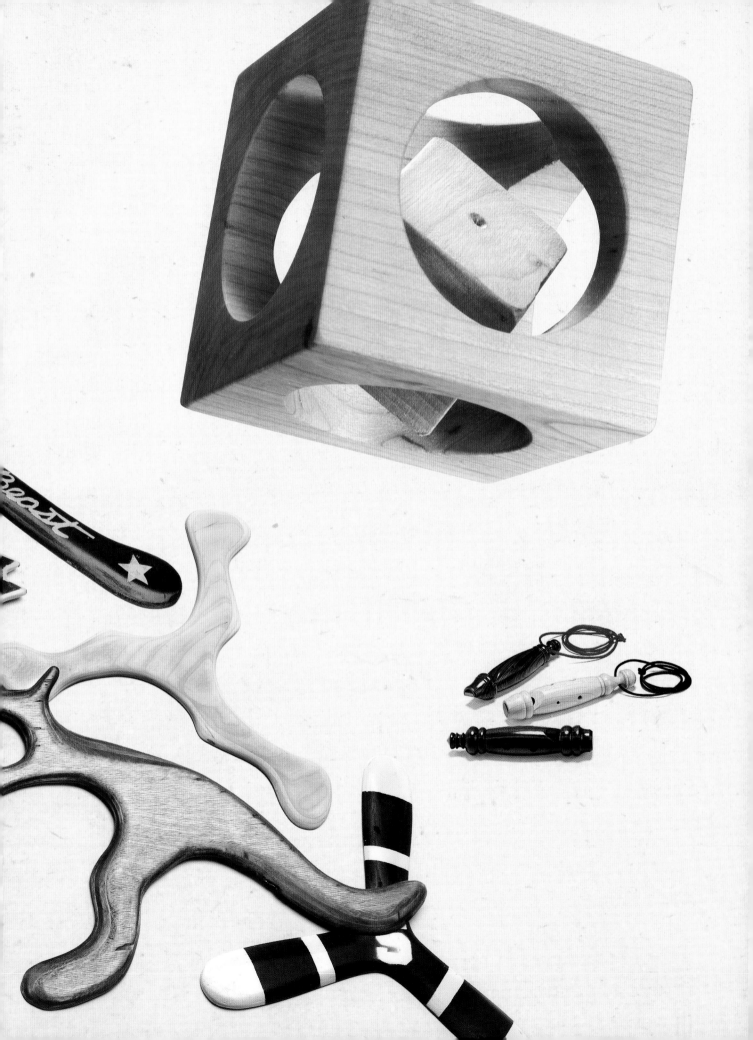

CHAPTER TEN
BUILD A BOOMERANG

by Trevor Smith

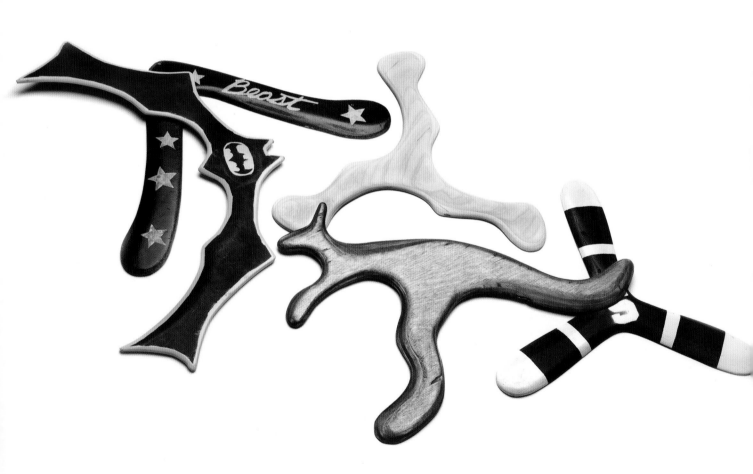

If you like a challenge, enjoy having an excuse to be outside and are looking for ideas for practical projects, you'll find that building a boomerang is great fun.

Also, boomerangs are a great project to build with family members you've wanted to introduce to woodworking. And when you are done you get to go to the park and spend time together throwing them.

I have just one warning: Boomerangs will draw a curious crowd of onlookers.

A LITTLE SCIENCE OF BOOMERANGS

Here's the first rule of boomerangs: Do not be afraid of trial and error. There are a wide variety of shapes that will work.

Boomerangs operate on the principle of gyroscopic precession, which is similar to riding a bike no handed and attempting to initiate a turn. In bike riding, the spinning (gyroscopic) motion of the wheels gives the bike stability. To execute a no-hands bicycle turn, you simply lean the bike in the direction that you wish to turn. The wheels have a delayed reaction to the force of the leaning action. This way, the wheels actually feel the force a quarter turn from where the force was applied. So instead of falling over, the bicycle turns in the desired direction.

Unlike riding a bicycle with no hands while turning, the boomerang experiences a continuous turn as the force is applied for the duration of the flight. The boomerang is thrown with a slight tilt from vertical (more on this later). The gyroscopic nature of a spinning boomerang and the release angle (called the layover angle) causes the boomerang's flight angle to flatten out as it turns. Thus a well-balanced, well-contoured and well-thrown boomerang will return to the thrower in a horizontal hover. For most people this will take practice though.

The duration of flight is determined by the force with which the boomerang was thrown as well as the spin applied at launch. As with any object flying through the air, a boomerang is subject to drag its own weight as it makes its flight pattern. This drag slows the boomerang down, thereby limiting the flight time. However, given enough spin and initial velocity, the boomerang will circle above the thrower's head a few times before landing.

CHOOSING A SHAPE & A MATERIAL

Even if you don't fully understand how boomerangs work, you can still make one that flies quite well. There are a wide variety of plans available on the Internet. Or you can start with the scaled plans here.

For your first boomerang, pick a simple design that will be easy to make and throw. It is best not to pick a complex design that is for trick flying.

My high school physics students love watching their classmates throw boomerangs almost as much as they enjoy throwing them.

Not only do you have to have a carefully made boomerang for success, but also good throwing form. Notice the pinch grip as this student prepares to release his boomerang into flight.

The traditional wood used by the aboriginal tribes of Australia to make boomerangs is myall brigalow (Acacia harpophylla). According to George Simonds Boulger in his book "Wood: A Manual of the Natural History and Industrial Applications of the Timber of Commerce" (BiblioLife), this native wood is "brown, strongly violet-scented, very heavy, very hard, elastic, durable, splitting freely. Used for turnery, tobacco-pipes, vine-stakes, spears and boomerangs."

A practical, quality and easy-to-work-with material for this project is plywood. However, the plywood at the big box stores isn't a good choice. Boomerangs are essentially flying wings, and better grades of plywood are more durable. In fact some plywoods are engineered for flying projects.

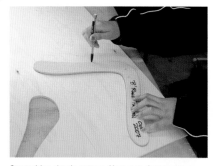

Start with a simple pattern. Here a student traces a bi-wing pattern onto ¼" plywood. The next step is to cut out the shape using some sort of saw that has the ability to cut curves.

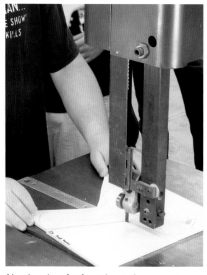

A band saw is perfect for cutting your boomerange shape. Here a student uses a large Powermatic band saw in the school shop.

A spindle sander is an efficient tool for smoothing the perimeter of the boomerang. Getting one smooth and fair line all the way around the boomerang is the goal at this stage.

When I teach high school physics students to build boomerangs, I prefer to use ¼"-thick Baltic birch or Finnish birch. Baltic birch costs less, but Finnish birch is laminated with waterproof glue so it can hold up better outdoors. The two plywoods are easy to tell apart. The glue lines for Baltic are similar in color to the wood. The waterproof glue used in Finnish birch is a dark chocolate color.

ROUGH OUT YOUR BOOMERANG

Once you have your wood and a pattern, you'll need to gather the tools. You need some sort of saw that can cut curves, such as a band saw, coping saw or bowsaw. To smooth the shape and thin the edges of your boomerang you need files and sandpaper. A spindle sander is nice to have, but it is not required.

If you are going to make several boomerangs in one shape, I recommend you make a pattern. We use paper bags, poster board or thin plastic sheeting.

Transfer the boomerang's shape to the wood blank. Then cut the shape out with your saw. I use this opportunity to teach the physics students how to use a band saw safely. Many students have never used power tools and this was a great way to introduce their safe use.

Once the shape of the boomerang is sawn out, you can refine its outline with a spindle sander or files and sandpaper.

SHAPING THE AIRFOIL

Now you need to make some important decisions. Like golf clubs, boomerangs are "handed." How the boomerang's airfoil is laid out and shaped depends on whether the person who is going to throw the boomerang is right-handed or left-handed.

The illustration on page 63 shows the airfoil shape of a right-handed boomerang. For a left-handed boomerang, you simply reverse the airfoil shape.

First mark the top of the boomerang. As with airplane wings, the airfoils on a boomerang have a leading and a trailing edge. The leading edge is a quarter-round shape and the trailing edge tapers off the top of the boomerang like the cross section of a typical airplane wing. Mark the two leading edges and the two trailing edges so you do not file them incorrectly (a common mistake my students make). The bottom face of the wing is completely flat.

Lay out the leading and trailing edges of the wings based on which hand will do the throwing. A marking gauge can be used for this (or the old trick of holding a finger against the edge). Mark in on the top the distance that the contour retreats back from the boomerang's edge to its top surface.

The quarter-round shape generally extends about ¼" from the edge, while the trailing edge extends about 1" to 1½" into the material. Note that you only have to shape

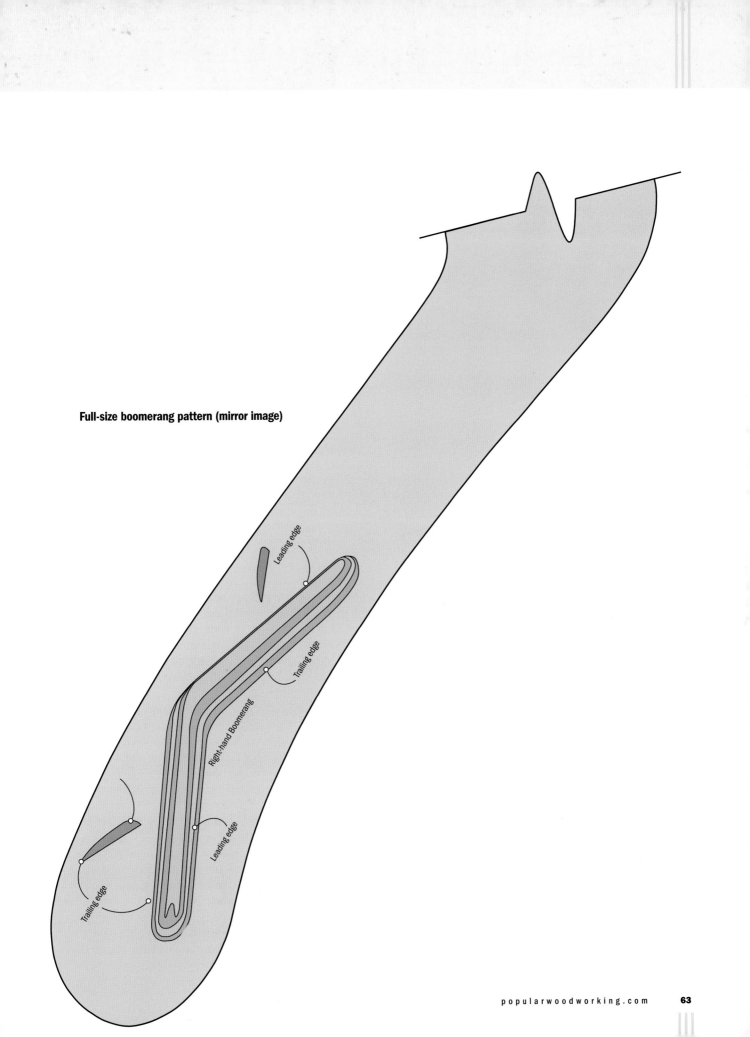

Full-size boomerang pattern (mirror image)

Leading edge

Trailing edge

Right-hand Boomerang

Leading edge

Trailing edge

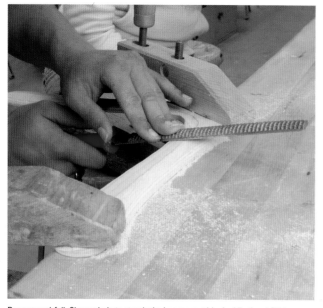

Rasp your airfoil. Clamps help to steady the boomerang blank while the airfoil is brought to life. Notice that the boomerang is positioned off the edge of the workbench so the the rasp does not damage the bench surface.

Fine-tune with sandpaper. After a couple test flights you'll want to add some refinement to the shape of the airfoils using some sandpaper.

one face of the plywood. The other face is left flat. See the illustration on page 63 to understand how the airfoil shape looks on a simple "V"-shaped boomerang. Note how the leading edge and trailing edge change along the length of the boomerang.

Shape the airfoil with rasps, files and sandpaper. There are a variety of rasps available out there. We used Nicholson cabinetmakers No. 49 and 50 cabinet rasps.

A boomerang is actually a flying rotating rotor, like on a helicopter. The airfoil shape needs to be consistent, and this is where the plys in plywood help in the design of the project. As the glue lines appear from the plys it is easy to observe the progress when shaping of the airfoils.

The optional finishing touch to shaping the airfoil is to slightly bevel the back edge of the wing. Or, another option is to make some test throws first and see if your boomerang is making a complete turn. If it is not, then file a slight back bevel on the flat face of the leading edge.

Before you decorate your boomerang, you should take it for a test spin because you might want to refine its airfoil.

THROWING TECHNIQUE

When teaching students to throw a boomerang, we start by using example boomerangs made with paper and cardboard in the classroom.

Throwing requires a little practice, so it is worth the time to make a few quick cardboard practice boomerangs. Cereal boxes are a great raw material for this. You can make a quick cardboard boomerang using two strips of cardboard approximately 1" wide and 8" to 10" long. Use hot-melt glue to form them into the shape of a plus sign. Put a gentle upward curl on the four blades and throw using the same techniques described below for throwing wooden boomerangs.

The throwing technique has a few key components, regardless of the material. Pinch the boomerang between your thumb and index finger and hold it over your head. Your thumb grasps the airfoil shape. The index finger is against the flat face of the boomerang.

Now hold your arm perfectly vertical. Before you throw, you need to tilt your arm 10° to 20° away from your body. This is called the layover angle. See the illustration on page 66 for what this looks like.

The throwing motion employs a lot of wrist action to generate the necessary spin around the center of mass of the thrown wing. Throw the boomerang at an angle of 45° from the front of the body. (That's with straight out in front being 0° and arms held straight out at the sides being 90°.) The angles are guidelines to get you started in the right direction. Do not be afraid to experiment with the throwing angles.

Here a student winds up to throw a tri-wing boomerang. Tri-wings spin very fast, but do not fly as far as the more traditional bi-wings.

When throwing a boomerang outside, the wind should be light and blowing straight into your face. The throw is still 45° from the front. Aim for a point about 10° above the horizon. This will send the boomerang flying. See the illustrations on the next page for details.

One of the important reasons to make indoor boomerangs before making wood ones is to learn the throwing motion. Indoors, the flight patterns are smaller, and the feedback for good and poor throws and working designs occurs quickly. The cardboard 'rangs are quite harmless if they hit someone too.

Once everyone is able to prove that they can throw a boomerang and not a "stick" or "kylie" (as a nonreturning boomerang is called in Australia), then it is time to find a place outside to throw your wooden version.

FIND A SPACE TO THROW

The larger the throwing area the better, especially when learning to throw. Parks are areas worth scouting. A foot-ball or soccer field is a good-size space to start with. There is less chance of losing a boomerang if the area is very large. Do not throw in an area where there are children, pets, cars or structures that may get in the way.

How to Throw a Boomerang

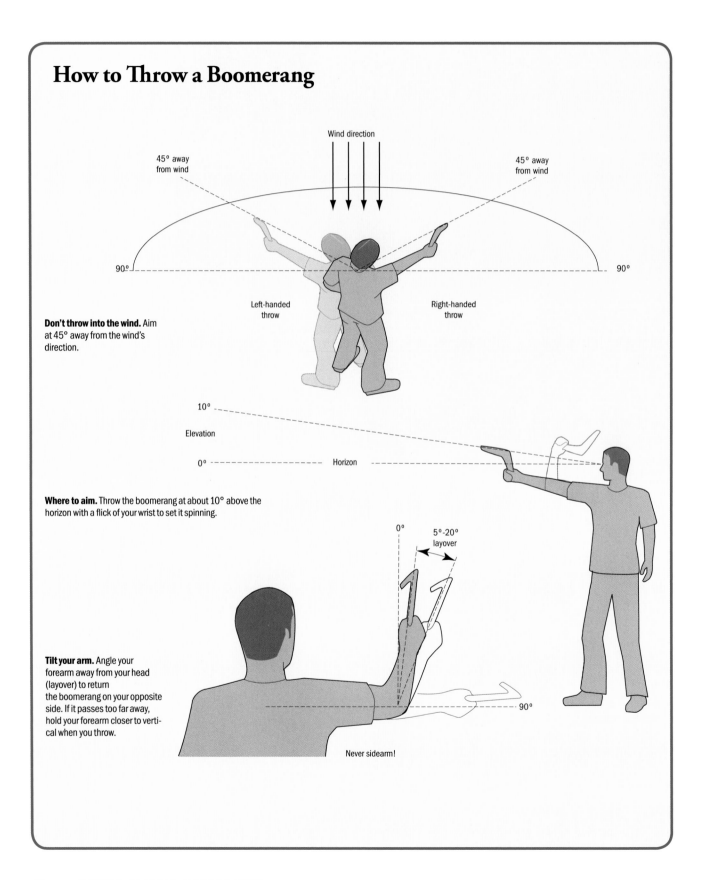

Wind direction

45° away from wind

45° away from wind

90°

90°

Left-handed throw

Right-handed throw

Don't throw into the wind. Aim at 45° away from the wind's direction.

10°

Elevation

0°   Horizon

Where to aim. Throw the boomerang at about 10° above the horizon with a flick of your wrist to set it spinning.

0°

5°-20° layover

Tilt your arm. Angle your forearm away from your head (layover) to return the boomerang on your opposite side. If it passes too far away, hold your forearm closer to vertical when you throw.

90°

Never sidearm!

CHAPTER ELEVEN

CLASSIC WOODEN BAT

by Alan Lacer

Major league bat

2¾" max

42" max, 32" - 36" typ.

Adult softball bat

2¼" max

34" max, 38 oz. max weight

Little League bat

2¼" max

33" max, 26" - 32" Typ.

FIG. A
Note: These numbers are only guidelines. Because of the ever-changing and sometimes localized nature of bat regulations, it's best to check with your local league officials for specific bat dimension limits.

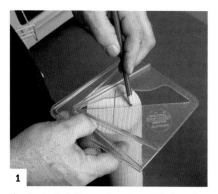

1

If you're starting with a purchased round blank, mark the center on both ends with a plastic center finder. On a square blank use a ruler across the diagonals to find the centers.

2

True the cylinder's entire length with a spindle-roughing gouge. This step is necessary because the blank may be warped, or your center marks aren't perfect. Take light cuts. You don't want to remove too much stock.

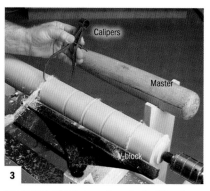

3

Size the bat with calipers and a parting tool. Transfer diameters from a drawing or an existing bat (called a master) onto the blank. Lightly push the calipers into the work as you reduce the diameter with the parting tool until the calipers just slip over the cut.

The crack of a baseball against a wooden bat is a wonderful sound seldom heard today. Too often it's been replaced by the metallic clink of an aluminum bat. Baseball has its roots in balls, gloves and shoes made from animal hides and bats made from trees. It seems an odd place for high tech equipment to intrude. Making a wooden bat returns you and your kids to the real, old-time baseball.

THE RIGHT WOOD

Almost every common wood has been used for bats at one time or another. However, a few species dominate the history of the sport. Traditionally northern ash has been the wood of choice, but currently – at least in the pros – it is a neck-and-neck race with hard maple. A few bats are still made of hickory and beech. For this project, I suggest buying a blank of ash or maple that has been graded for bats (see Sources, page 71). The reason is not only superior performance, but also safety. A bat made from a graded bat blank is less likely to break in use.

Bat blanks are graded differently from regular furniture grade lumber. First, only straight-grained wood from slow-growing trees of moderate size make the grade. The blank must have tight, evenly spaced growth rings and be free of flaws like knots. The best blanks are often split from the log rather than sawn in order to follow the grain perfectly. Extra care is taken in the drying of bat blanks to create an even distribution of moisture throughout the entire thickness.

TOOLS & SUPPLIES

To make a full-size baseball bat you will need a lathe that can handle lengths up to 36" between centers. For Little League bats a lathe with shorter capacity will work just fine. It is best to have a live center at the tailstock end, and drive with either a spur or cup drive. If you are duplicating a bat, you will need to fabricate a simple V-block system to hold the master bat (the one being duplicated) directly behind your blank (**Photo 3**).

The bat can be turned with three tools: a spindle-roughing gouge (1¼" to 1¾"), a parting tool (¼" wide) and a spindle/detail gouge (⅜" or ½"). If you are comfortable using a skew, a large one (1" to 1½") can be added as an option for smoothing the shape and rounding the end of the barrel.

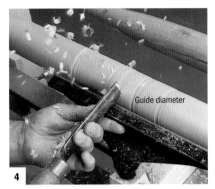

4

Use a spindle-roughing gouge to connect the dots. The goal is to join and blend the different guide diameters to create a smooth cylinder that tapers towards the handle.

5

Take light cuts and create level transitions as you approach the final shape of the barrel. Work from the large diameter to the small to minimize tear-out.

6

Roll over the end of the barrel with a detail/spindle gouge. Shoot for a smooth, gradual curve like the master has. Leave about a ½" x 2" diameter waste area near your live center for now.

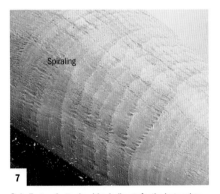

7

Spiraling or chatter is a big challenge for the bat maker. Spiraling results from the wood flexing, or the tool bouncing or a combination of both. As the bat gets thinner, the problem becomes more pronounced.

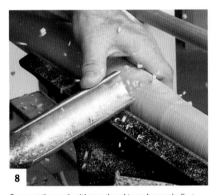

8

Support the work with your hand to reduce spiraling. This is a safe and common practice. Make sure there is little gap between the tool rest and the wood. Keep your hand pressure on the back of the blank.

9

A steady rest is an alternative to the hand-support method. It virtually eliminates chatter and spiraling because the work is supported on three sides at once. A steady rest requires a smooth area for the wheels to run upon.

Complete your supplies with a pair of locking outside calipers. Make sure the caliper's points are fully rounded smooth. Sharp points can catch when used to size your bat. Round the points with a file and smooth with sandpaper. A pair of dividers is helpful – although optional – for sizing the knob's width. A plastic center finder is helpful in locating centers on round bat blanks (see Sources).

PREPARE THE BLANK

Determine the type of the bat you intend to turn: Major League, softball or Little League. This can be based on an old favorite you'd like to duplicate or from scratch using a drawing based on regulations dimension (see **Fig. A**, page 68). The blank should be 1" to 2" longer than the finished bat to allow for waste at both ends.

Mark the centers on the blank (**Photo 1**) and mount it on the lathe. I place the barrel end of the bat at the tailstock. Then I true the cylinder to the axis of the lathe (**Photo 2**).

SHAPE THE BARREL

Shape the widest part of the bat, called the barrel, first. You want to preserve the thick diameter on the blank as long as possible to avoid chatter from vibration. Start by making guide diameters on the first third of the blank with calipers and a parting tool (**Photo 3**). Set the calipers about ⅛" wider than the desired diameter to allow for final shaping and sanding. If you're duplicating a bat, place the master directly behind the mounted blank.

Next is a process of connecting the guide diameters with the spindle-roughing gouge (**Photo 4**). Shoot for smooth transitions between the guide diameters (**Photo 5**).

Go ahead and roll over the end of the barrel at this time (**Photo 6**).

SHAPE THE HANDLE

Mark and shape the middle third of the bat in the same way you shaped the barrel. When you reach the last third

10 Work the area to the right of the knob. Cut from the large diameter towards the small diameter (also known as cutting downhill). This produces the smoothest cut with the least tear-out.

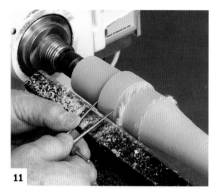

11 Establish the width of the knob with a pair of dividers. I keep the wood on either side of the knob as fat as possible until the handle area is almost complete. This helps reduce spiraling from a flexing blank.

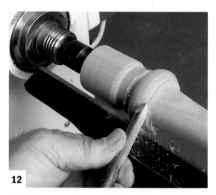

12 Roll the knob using the spindle/detail gouge. Start at the widest portion of the knob and ride the bevel of the gouge down to the handle or waste block. The open or U-shaped portion of the gouge faces the direction of the cut.

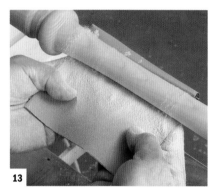

13 Sand your bat with the tool rest, steady rest and master bat removed. Start with #100-grit followed by #120, #150 and #180-grit paper.

14 Add a customized look to your bat by burning in your own brand. The brand is always placed on the face grain portion of the bat to give the hitter a point of reference for positioning the bat.

15 Apply a finish to give a richer look to the bat as well as some protection against moisture.

of the bat, remove some of the waste material towards the knob end first to give you some working room. Spindle work is best done from larger to smaller diameters because it produces the least amount of tearout. As you reduce the diameter of the bat, you will experience chatter. This usually shows up as spiral marks on the surface of the wood (**Photo 7**). To reduce chatter, use a sharp tool and keep it firmly planted on the tool rest. Take light cuts. Avoid pushing hard or you're bound to get chatter from the flexing blank. Even with all these tactics, you will need added support as the handle narrows. The traditional method is to support the narrow area with your hand (**Photo 8**). Another option is to employ a steady rest (**Photo 9**). I use a steady rest when I get to about the middle of the blank.

Continue the process of cutting and connecting the guide diameters working from the large diameters on either end towards the narrowest point on the handle (**Photo 10**).

SHAPE THE KNOB

As you approach the end of the bat, go ahead and lay out the knob area. Establish the knob's width and diameter (**Photo 11**). Then reduce the diameter on the knob's right side, blending into the handle. Leave a ½" to 1" length of waste material past the end of the knob.

After the handle area is completed, finish off the knob by rolling away the corners with the spindle/detail gouge (**Photo 12**).

FINISHING TOUCHES

Sand the entire piece, working through the different grits up to #180 (**Photo 13**). Turn the waste material on both ends down to slightly larger than your lathe centers. Remove the bat, cut the waste off with a handsaw (such as a small Japanese saw), and finish sanding the ends of your bat by hand or a disc on the lathe.

Most bats have brands to indicate how the bat should be held. Always swing the bat with the label up to reduce the chances of breakage.

The goal is to hit the ball on the radial grain, or what some woodworkers call the edge grain – rather than the tangential or face grain. So, put your brand on the grain that looks like chevrons rather than the edges of plywood. Use a woodburning tool to put whatever name or symbol you wish to use as your brand (**Photo 14**).

I recommend finishing your bat (**Photo 15**). A finish gives the bat a nicer look as it brings out the grain. Plus it offers some protection from moisture. All types of finishes have been used for bats, including shellac, lacquer, varnish (water-based or oil-based). For this bat I am using a wipe-on poly; three coats is sufficient. Some players prefer the handle area to be free of finish – for better gripping and applying pine tar.

Now, it's time to hit the field!

SOURCES

Craft Supplies
woodturnerscatalog.com
800 551 8876
ash bat blanks #104-359 $18.95 or #25.95 in hard maple; woodburner #1040671 $85.95 (other models available).

Oneway
oneway.ca
800 565 7288
Spindle steady #3280, $144.95.

CHAPTER TWELVE
FANCY WHISTLE

by Steve Blenk

This little gem is called an ocarina because it plays eight notes. The turning is simple so you'll probably spend more time off the lathe drilling, sawing and fitting the parts. Even so, you can make this ocarina in less than an hour. I'll show you how to turn it, make it whistle and play a tune.

PREPARE THE BLANK

You can use any hardwood that cuts cleanly – I've made these whistles out of everything from maple to rosewood, and they all seem to work well. Avoid softwoods, though. They absorb moisture and that affects tone quality. These whistles are so quick to turn that I usually make them in multiples, starting by cutting a length of 1¼" square stock into 5" lengths.

Drill a ½" diameter hole in the end of each blank to a depth of 3¾". Keeping this hole precisely centered in the blank is not critical, but try to keep it close!

MAKE THE MANDRELS

The end-bored blank gets mounted on a wooden shaft for working. This shaft is called a mandrel. Turn your own ½"

diameter mandrels – about 2" long – from solid stock. You'll need one lathe-mounted mandrel for turning (**Photo 1**), and another turned on the end of a square section so you can hold the whistle level for sawing, sanding and drilling (**Photo 4**).

TURN THE WHISTLE

Once the blank is mounted and turned round, the only precise lathe work is the cut that defines the whistle's mouthpiece (**Fig. A**). The placement and depth of this cut, 1" from the squared open end, to a point (not a flat) at ¾" diameter affects the whistle's tuning (**Photo 2**).

Turn the body of the whistle as any spindle, but remember that most of it has a hollowed center. You can only make deep decorative cuts at the solid end.

Before removing the piece from the lathe, locate positions for the tone holes (**Photo 3**).

CUT OUT THE MOUTH

The whistle's mouth is a notch cut to expose the center bore at a 60° angle. I make this cut on the bandsaw using a

Fig A. Side and top views
Shape the whistle's body around these important dimensions

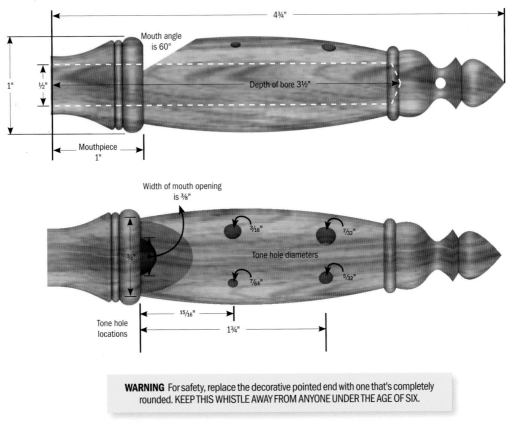

WARNING For safety, replace the decorative pointed end with one that's completely rounded. KEEP THIS WHISTLE AWAY FROM ANYONE UNDER THE AGE OF SIX.

1

Slide the end-bored blank onto a wooden mandrel of the same diameter, mounted on the lathe. Support the blank from the tail stock with a live center. Turn it round to about 1" diameter, then square the bored end, leaving a bore length of 3½".

2

Shape the shoulder of the mouthpiece so it ends in a point (Fig. A) by cutting in with a parting tool held at an angle. Start beyond the mark that locates the end of the mouthpiece and work back to it, turning the tool inward as you define the shoulder and deepen the cut.

3

Mark positions for the tone holes (Fig. A) by drawing rings around the turned whistle body. Before drilling (Photo 7), mark points on these rings to locate the four holes.

14-tpi blade with the whistle mounted on a mandrel block (**Photo 4**). After cutting, refine and smooth the surface with fine sandpaper glued onto an angled sanding block (**Photo 5**).

MAKE A FIPPLE

A fipple is a dowel with a tapered, flattened side. Position the fipple in the mouthpiece of the whistle with its flat side parallel to the mouth opening and its front edge barely protruding into it. Test the sound. You can adjust the tone by moving the fipple in or out. Once you've achieved a good clear tone, mark the block so you can accurately reposition it. Then remove it and set it aside.

MAKE SOME MUSIC

This whistle has four tone holes, two on each side of its body. Each one of them has a different diameter so that when covered singly or in combination, you can play eight different notes. Locate the holes so the whistle is convenient to hold while playing (**Photo 3**). Drill the holes at the drill press with the whistle again mounted on the mandrel block (**Photo 7**). The diameters of the holes are critical to the tones, so use the correct size bits (**Fig. A**). Clean out any waste that is clinging to the inner bore of the whistle with sandpaper.

Remount the fipple in the mouthpiece and check the tone of each note. Making a hole slightly larger (by filing or sanding) will lower the pitch. If you need to make the hole smaller to raise the pitch, try a bit of epoxy around its edge, or plug it and redrill.

When you are satisfied with the tone, glue the fipple in place. Be sure that its flat surface is parallel to the mouth

opening, and that its front edge extends a tiny bit into the vertical cut of the mouth (**Fig. B**). Test the tone, again, to make sure everything is properly positioned before the glue sets.

After the glue on the fipple has set, cut off the extra length from the front of the mouthpiece and sand it smooth. Then use a sanding drum chucked in a drill press

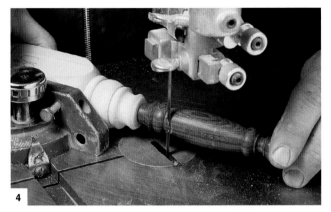

4

Cut the whistle's mouth on the bandsaw. Hold the whistle on a mandrel turned on the end of a square section. Make the first cut with the miter gauge reversed and set at 30°, to give a 60° cut. Make this cut in the quarter-sawn grain of the whistle, starting about ½". from the mouthpiece shoulder. The second cut is at 90°, right at the shoulder (Fig. A). These cuts expose the center bore.

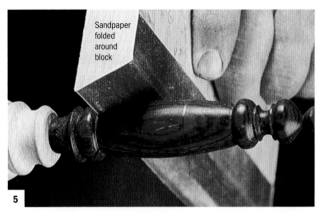

Sandpaper folded around block

5

Sand both surfaces of the whistle's mouth with sandpaper folded around a 60° angle block so they meet in a smooth, crisp line. The angled surface must be dead flat, so clamp the mandrel firmly on a hard surface and pull the block toward you. Don't sand back and forth. When you're finished, the exposed bore should measure ⅜" at its widest point.

6

Make a cedar fipple, a ½" diameter round dowel with one side sanded flat and tapered. It fits into the mouthpiece and directs the air blown into the whistle. Getting the right size and taper (Fig. B) is an inexact science, so you may have to make and test several fipples to get one that makes a clear tone. Make them long, about 1¼", so they're easy to reposition or replace.

30°

7

Drill tone holes in the whistle about 30° from the top of the center axis. A mandrel long enough to extend beyond the drilling points will minimize tear-out on the inside. Chamfer the outer surfaces of the holes slightly to help your fingers make contact and a good seal. After drilling, sand the inside with a rolled piece of #220-grit sandpaper, but don't enlarge the bore. If you do, the fipple won't fit.

Fig. B
Fitting the Fipple

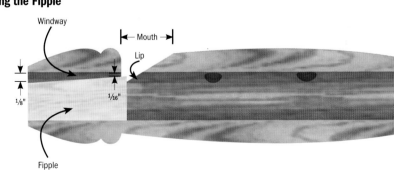

Windway

Mouth

Lip

⅛"

1/16"

Fipple

When fitted inside the whistle's mouthpiece, the flattened side of the fipple forms a windway. Air blown through it is accelerated by the narrowing passage and directed at the mouth's lip as it exits. The mouth's lip splits the blown air, directing it into the bored-out center and creating the whistle's sound. Minute adjustments to any part change the flow of the air and affect the sound.

8

Shape the mouthpiece (Fig. B) after gluing the fipple in place. A sanding drum creates a concave shape that looks good and sounds good, too.

to shape the bottom of the mouthpiece (**Photo 8**). If you plan to drill the tail end for a string, this is the time to do it.

Finish the whistle with multiple light coats of spray lacquer. A long screw mounted through the hole for the string makes it convenient to hold the whistle while finishing. Allow the lacquer to cure fully before playing. It's hard to play sweet music on a sour-tasting instrument! Do plan on making these little gems in batches because every time you play yours in public you will be asked to make more!

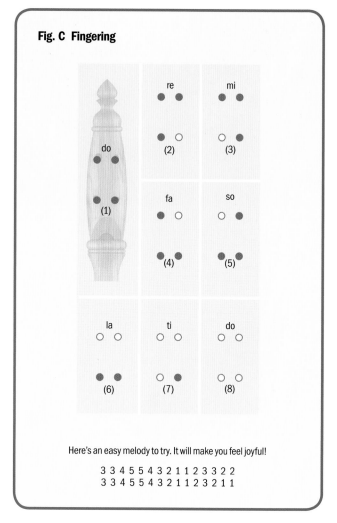

Fig. C Fingering

Here's an easy melody to try. It will make you feel joyful!

3 3 4 5 5 4 3 2 1 1 2 3 3 2 2
3 3 4 5 5 4 3 2 1 1 2 3 2 1 1

CHAPTER THIRTEEN
JACOB'S LADDER

by A.J. Hamler

1

Sand each block smooth, and use the sanding block to lightly round all edges.

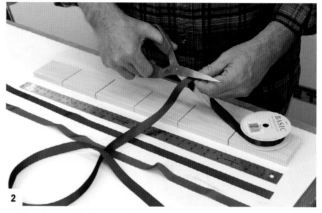

2

Cut three ribbons, allowing several extra inches for each.

3

Glue the single center ribbon to the first block.

4

Tack the center ribbon into place.

When I was a kid I was fascinated by a toy called Jacob's Ladder, although I didn't know at the time that's what it was called. My name for them was "tumble blocks," and it's easy to see why I thought that. When held by one of the end blocks and dangled, the blocks hang down in a straight line. Tilt that top block forward and over, and each block in turn flips all the way down, clacking delightfully as they go. Tilt that top block back the other way and the blocks flip all the way down again.

The Jacob's Ladder has been a popular toy for a few centuries (*Scientific American* published an article on it back in 1889), but don't ask me to explain how it works; I can't. What I do know is that if you attach the ribbons to six blocks in the right spots the tumbling action works all on its own, which is enough explanation for me.

To make one you'll need a piece of ½" thick by 2½" wide stock; any standard ½" x 3" material, which is really 2½" wide, will do. I chose poplar because I like the sharper clacking sound you get from hardwood, but pine clacks fine.

BUILDING JACOB'S LADDER

Cut six 4" pieces by your preferred method, then give them a good sanding (**Photo 1**). Start with #100-grit paper, then bump up to #150- or #180-grit to make them nice and smooth. Round over all the sharp edges a bit, particularly

CUTTING LIST

Overall dimensions extended: 2½" wide x ½" thick x 24¼" long; stacked: 2½" wide x 4" long x 3⅛" high

Ref	Qty.	Part	Stock	Dimensions (T, W, L)		
A	6	Block	Poplar	½"	2½"	4"

ADDITIONAL MATERIALS

#6 x ½" tacks (18 needed)
½" or ⅝" ribbon (3 pieces needed, approximately 30" each)
High-tack craft glue

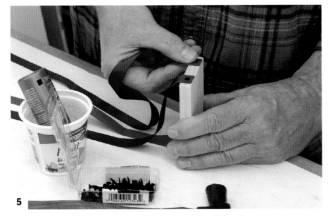

5 Flip the first block over, then glue and tack the two outer ribbons into place.

6 Lay the first block flat, and fold the ribbons over the top.

7 Lay the second block atop the first, and apply glue on the ends above the ribbons.

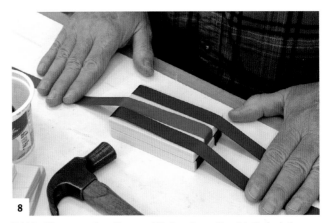

8 Fold the ribbons up and over the second block, and press them into the fresh glue.

on the ends so they'll tumble freely without snagging on one another.

Combining the length of the six 4" blocks and accounting for a slight gap between them, the ladder is slightly over 24" long. Cut three pieces of ½" or ⅝" ribbon to about 30" to give you plenty of working length, as in **Photo 2**. We'll trim off any extra later. I chose blue for the outer ribbons and red for the center one, but get any color ribbon you like.

To get the hinging action between the blocks correct, attach the ribbons in order beginning with the bottom block. Start by attaching the end of the center ribbon – the red one in these photos – to the center of the bottom block, as in **Photo 3**. Use a high-tack craft glue to position the ribbon. High-tack glue has a very short open time and grabs hold very quickly, which simplifies assembly.

Hold the ribbon firmly in place for about half a minute, then secure it permanently with a #6 x ½" tack (**Photo 4**). Be careful when working with tacks. They're extremely sharp.

Flip the block over and attach the two outer ribbons (blue here) with glue and tacks in the same manner, taking care that the ribbons go the same direction (**Photo 5**). By the way, in these photos you'll notice that I've got the glue upside down in a small cup. That's because craft glue is very thick, and keeping it upside down in the cup keeps the glue ready to go at the top of the bottle. Much easier than shaking it down every time.

With the ribbons attached, lay the first block on your work surface and fold the ribbons over the top, as in **Photo 6**. Now place the second block atop the folded ribbons on the first and apply glue on the ends just above the three ribbons below the new block, as shown in **Photo 7**. That'll be one dab of glue on the end over the center ribbon, and two dabs on the end with the two outer ribbons. Fold those ribbons up and press them into the glue, holding them in place for about 30 seconds so the glue can grab (**Photo 8**). When folding the ribbons up, do so lightly. The blocks need a bit of wiggle room between them to function properly, so you don't want to pull them tight.

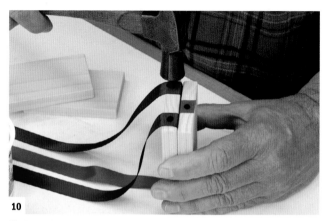

9 Once the glue has had a chance to grab, upend the blocks and tack the center ribbon securely.

10 Flip the two blocks over, then glue and tack the outer ribbons into place as before.

11 Fold the ribbons over the top, then lay the third block atop the second and apply glue as before.

12 Once the stack is complete, trim the ribbons flush with the top block.

Upend the stack and tack the center ribbon into place, as in **Photo 9**, then flip the stack and do the same with the outer ribbons on the other end (**Photo 10**).

From this point forward it's just a matter of repeating the steps and building the stack. With the ribbons tacked on the second block, lay the stack down as before, fold the ribbons over the top, lay the third block into place and dab glue at the ribbon attachment points. If you compare **Photo 11** with the similar step shown in **Photo 7**, you can see that the ribbons are now oriented in the opposite direction – the center ribbon goes to the left here and the outer ones to the right. This should alternate as you work your way up the stack and is a good way to keep track of those ribbons. With the glue applied, fold the ribbons up and press them into the glue, then follow with tacks as before and the third block is complete.

Now just add the fourth, fifth and sixth blocks, repeating the process of gluing and tacking the ribbons in place

each time. When you've reached the top of the stack and have the ribbon secured to the last block, trim the excess ribbon with scissors (**Photo 12**).

Kids can customize the Jacob's Ladder in a number of ways. Changing the ribbon color is an obvious option, but you can also paint the blocks a variety of colors before assembly begins. Alternating colors on one side to the other completely changes the look of the ladder as the blocks tumble. If your kids are into art – and what kids aren't? – they can draw or paint designs, animals or anything else they like on the faces. I recently saw an interesting Jacob's Ladder where the young builder applied stick-on photos of all the Harry Potter villains on one side, and the Potter good guys on the other. Tumbling the blocks changed the ladder from the Dark Arts to Good Magic with the flip of the wrist.

CHAPTER FOURTEEN
YOUR FIRST TOOLBOX

by Joe Hurst-Wajszczuk

I'm sure I'm like most uncles when I say this, but Samuel was never like other 2-year-olds. Sure, he liked the taste of a good book, but he also spent hours staring at the construction drawings in his dad's woodworking books and magazines. To encourage the little craftsman, I built this toolbox and starter tool set. After finishing the set, I realized that a few of his tools not only looked better, but were more comfortable to hold than my own.

Although the tools shown here were designed for a child, I'm guessing that you may also know a few adults who wouldn't mind having a set like this decorating their desk. You can also use the toy plans to upgrade your own tools. For example, you can enlarge the saw pattern to fit your hand, and use a band saw to cut the kerf for a metal blade. A slightly beefier mallet would be perfect for assembling joints.

This is a perfect opportunity to use scraps that you've been hoarding for a special occasion. Just make sure to choose woods that won't splinter in case your craftsman gets a little too zealous. You might even want to consider a small production run – one for you and one to give away.

START WITH THE BOX

To build the toolbox, start by cutting the ends to size, then making a ⅜"-deep dado along the inside face of the end pieces to hold the bottom of the box. I nibbled out the groove by raising the cutting depth on my sliding compound miter saw and making repeated passes, but you could also use a table saw with a dado blade or a router with a straight bit. Now drill the handle holes and nip off the top corners at the angle shown. Lastly, use a router to round over both faces of the top end and the tapered edge.

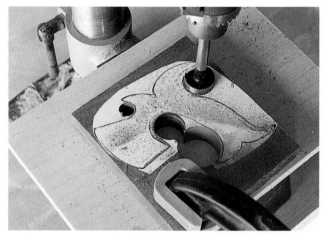

Use Forstner bits to make perfectly radiused curves. Connect the holes using your band saw, and you are halfway there.

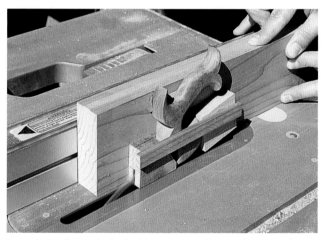

Secure the handle to the kerfing jig with carpet tape and hot glue. Glue a scrap from the handle blank in front of the handle to double-check the position of the blade.

Toolbox profile

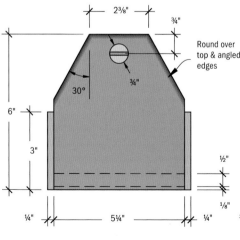

2⅜"   ¾"

Round over top & angled edges

¾"

30°

6"

3"

½"

¼"   5¼"   ¼"

⅛"

Toolbox elevation

14"

⅜"   13¼"   ⅜"

After cutting out the bottom and end pieces, consider investing a little time in sanding before assembly (it's a lot easier to sand now than it will be later). Assemble the box using glue and clamps.

Hold off on the brass nails until you've completely sanded and put the first coat of finish on the box. It's too easy to sand through the nails' thin brass plating.

Now it's time to attach the handle. Wedged tenons are an attractive and rock-solid way to attach the handle into the ends. Make sure to cut the wedge across, rather than parallel to, the end grain so that the dowel doesn't split when you drive in the wedge. It also helps to cut the wedge long, so that you can trim back the tapered end in case you need the dowel to flare more to fit the hole. Rub glue onto the outside of the dowel where it contacts the end pieces and to the faces of the wedges. Then tap the wedges in place. Wipe off any excess glue right away, but wait until the glue is dry before trimming the wedge with a dovetail or flush-cut saw.

THE SAW & SQUARE

The saw looks like an antique, and it feels like it was made for your hand (which it is), but it's no more difficult to make than a scroll-sawn duck. Simply copy the pattern on the right, affix it to a suitable piece of scrap, and start cutting. To make things even easier, I

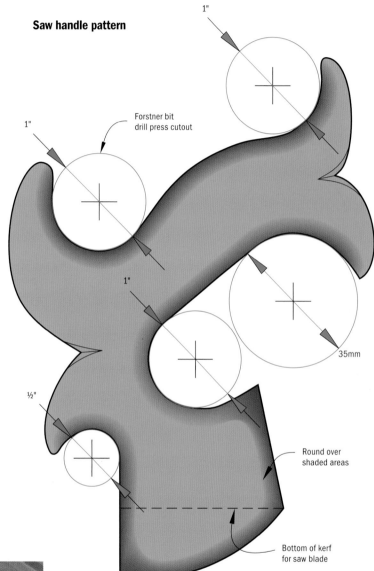

Saw handle pattern

1"

Forstner bit drill press cutout

1"

1"

½"

35mm

Round over shaded areas

Bottom of kerf for saw blade

Back your sandpaper to smooth the curves. Old mouse pads and carpet padding make excellent custom sanding pads.

used my drill press to make the curves, then connected the holes with my band saw. After cutting the basic shape, use a rasp to smooth out any major bumps. Then use your router to round over just the areas indicated on the drawing. To keep your fingers safely away from the bit, consider hot-gluing a handle to the saw handle before you rout.

Next cut the kerf for the blade. To do this, I made a simple kerfing jig from a scrap of 2x6 lumber. I attached the handle and the stops to the board with carpet tape and hot glue. As you can see in the photo above, the front stop was made from a leftover scrap from making the handle. I used this stop not only to secure the handle but also to mark out the slot for the blade. The straight-edged stop is much easier

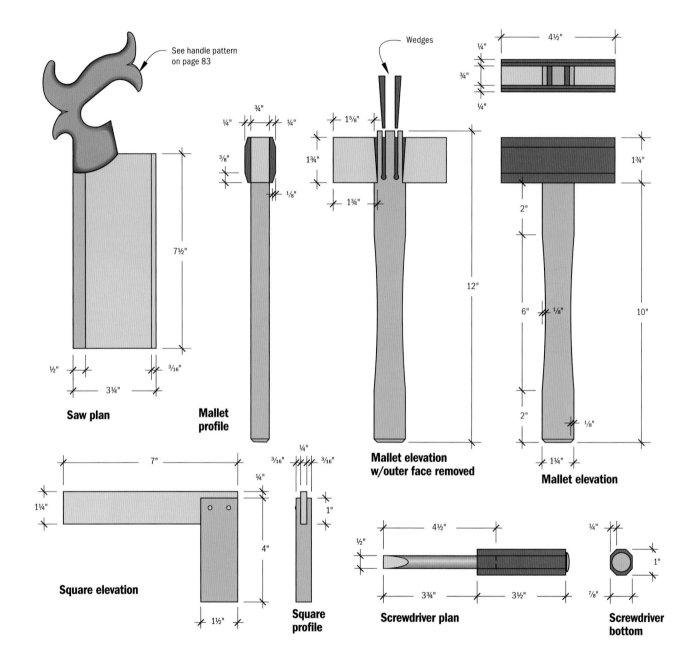

See handle pattern
on page 83

Wedges

4½"

¼"

¾"

¼"

¾"

¼"

¼"

1⁵⁄₈"

1¾"

1¾"

1¾"

7½"

12"

2"

6"

¹⁄₈"

10"

½"

3⁄16"

3¼"

2"

¹⁄₈"

Saw plan

**Mallet
profile**

**Mallet elevation
w/outer face removed**

1¼"

Mallet elevation

7"

¼"

3⁄16"

3⁄16"

¼"

1"

1¼"

4"

Square elevation

1½"

**Square
profile**

4½"

½"

¼"

1"

3¾"

3½"

⁷⁄₈"

Screwdriver plan

**Screwdriver
bottom**

to mark out than on the curved handle. Marking out the stop instead of the handle also gave me advanced warning if the fence or blade were not set correctly.

The last, but most important, step in building the handle is sanding. To help me get into the tight curves, I used a variety of materials. Cork, carpet padding and old mouse pads are some of my favorites. Wipe on a light coat of oil or mineral spirits to make any spots you've missed stand out.

Now it's time to shift focus to the blade. To make the backer strip, I used a shop-made scratch stock by filing the head of a screw to a point, then screwing it into a small block of wood. If you like, you can use spray paint or metal leaf to make the backer look like the real thing. Next I planed a small bevel on the opposite edge to represent teeth. (Don't think of filing "pretend" teeth on the saw. I discovered that a maple blade can saw through a pine table leg.) Once you've finished the blade, apply a small amount of glue and insert it into the handle.

You can shape the handle with a spokeshave in less time than it takes to read this chapter. By clamping the handle as shown, you can spin the handle to quickly round over all four edges.

When drilling into end grain, you can't use too many clamps. The stop also ensures that the small piece is perpendicular to the table.

Clip the heads off of staples to prevent the laminations from slipping during glue-up.

CUTTING LIST

No.	Item	Dimensions (inches)			Material
		T	W	L	
Toolbox					
2	Ends	¾	5¼	6	Walnut
2	Sides	¼	3	14	Oak
1	Bottom	½	5¼	13¼	Birch plywood
1	Handle	¾-dia.		14	Oak dowel
2	Wedges	¾	1		Walnut
Saw					
1	Handle	¾	3⅞	5½	Walnut
1	Blade	¼	3¼	7½	Maple
Square					
1	Handle	⅝	1½	4	Cherry
1	Blade	¼	1¼	7	Maple
Screwdriver					
1	Handle*	⅞	1	4	Padauk
1	End cap	¾-dia.			Maple round head plug
1	Blade	½-dia.		4½	Maple dowel
Mallet					
2	Head outer face	¼	1¾	4½	Padauk
2	Head core	¾	1¾	1¾	Oak
2	Wedges	¾		2	Padauk
1	Handle*	¾	1¼	12	Oak

*Dimension is long, trim to finished size

Once you've built the saw, the square is a piece of cake. Cut the pieces to size, kerf the handle, and glue the blade in place. Sand, finish and add the brass nails.

SCREWDRIVER

The screwdriver is made up of just three parts: the handle, the blade (a ½"-diameter dowel rod), and the end cap (made from a round head plug I found at my local craft store). The hardest part of making this tool is accurately drilling the ends of the handle. Starting with rectangular stock, cut the handle about ½" longer than you need. To locate the center of the handle, draw diagonals from corner to corner on both ends of the handle. An easy way to do this is by connecting opposite corners using a wide chisel and giving it a tap to establish the line.

After establishing the center point, drill the holes for the blade and cap. When drilling small stock it's important to clamp the wood in place. To provide something to clamp to, I made a simple clamping jig. After drilling the holes in both ends, insert the end cap, tilt your table saw's blade to 45° and trim off the corners to make the handle octagon. Just make sure that you don't cut into the cap. Next trim the handle to length and glue in the blade and end cap. Lastly, shape the tip of the blade on a belt sander or with a chisel.

MALLET

Rather than attempting to mortise the head of the mallet, I made a simple three-ply lamination. Laminating the head is an easy way to make a tapered mortise that guarantees that the handle will never come loose.

First, cut all the pieces to size. Remember to cut a small bevel of about 2° on the inside edges of the core pieces. Make the core and handle from the same stock to ensure a perfect fit. (Consider making the head's outer laminations thicker for a wider striking surface.) Next, use your table saw and kerfing jig to cut the slots in the handle for the wedges and two small steps along the outside edges. The steps stop the handle when it's inserted into the head. Drill holes in the bottom of the kerfs for the wedges so that you don't split the handle.

Shaping the handle is easier to do before it's attached to the head. Clamp the handle blank as shown below and use a spokeshave or file to knock off any sharp corners until you've got a comfortable handle. Finish up the handle with a light sanding.

When gluing the head together, position the core pieces so that their bottom edge touches the handle. There should be about a ⅛" gap between the end of the core piece and the top edge of the handle. To prevent the core from slipping during glue-up, I drove staples into each lamination, and then clipped off the heads so that the tip remained as shown below.

When the mallet head has dried, use your chop saw or table saw to trim off any squeeze-out and bevel the head. Bevel only the outer lamination; otherwise the handle will stick out past the head. Now you can insert the handle and glue in the wedges. Try to tap in the wedges the same amount so that when they're trimmed you get an even stripe pattern on the top of the mallet.

If you're making this tool set for a child, I recommend padding the mallet's ends with leather or cork. (Don't ask me how I know this. Sorry about the tub, Dave.) Cut the pads slightly oversized and attach them to the head with contact adhesive. Trim the caps to size after they're in place.

FINISHING

Because I wanted to make tools that begged to be touched, finishing took almost as long as building the pieces did in the first place. But I think the results were worth the extra effort.

First, sand everything down to #600-grit. This isn't as tedious as it sounds. Careful planing and scraping can help you jump straight to #320-grit. In fact, the padauk looked better after scraping than it did after sanding.

To bring out the grain, start with an oil finish. Once the oil has cured – use the applicator rags as a guide – apply a few coats of wipe-on polyurethane for extra protection. Don't apply poly to the padauk; the oils in the wood will prevent the finish from curing. Finally, rub on a coat of wax with an ultrafine (white) abrasive pad for extra shine.

CHAPTER FIFTEEN

CUBE IN A CUBE

by Jock Holmen

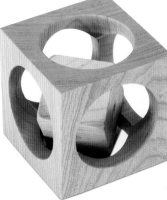

1

Crosscut a 3" x 3" x 14" blank into four cubes. Solid wood is best, so it doesn't look like you put the little cube in the big cube by gluing parts together. Table-leg stock works well, but you can make the cubes from smaller stock if you want.

2

Mark centerlines on one face. Mark one corner of every face with a small X. You'll be drilling each hole more than one time. The Xs will help register the cube in the same orientation on the drill press.

I'm a carver. I've always admired whittled curiosities like balls trapped inside a cage, but I never wanted to spend the time to make them. I figured there must be some way to make a similar object with a drill press — and I made this cube in a cube. Kids simply play with it, but it drives adults nuts. They think it's a puzzle. They're sure there's some way to get the little cube out of the big cube. (You can't — but don't tell them that.)

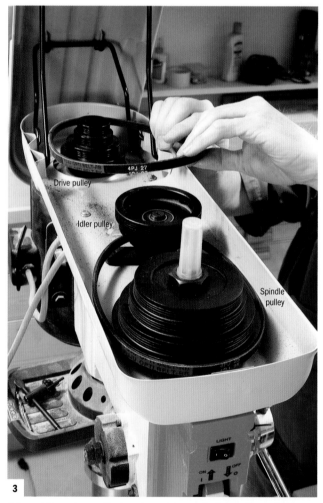

3

Set your drill press to run at its slowest speed. Arrange the belts so the smallest diameter drive pulley turns the idler pulley. Connect the idler to the largest diameter spindle pulley.

4

Set up your drill press with a 2" Forstner bit. (Use a smaller bit with a smaller block.) Position a fence and stop-block so the bit drills exactly in the cube's center. Drill one hole about 1/16" deep.

5

Set the bit's depth of cut. Draw a line from the point where a diagonal intersects the hole you made. Adjust the drill press so the bit stops about 1/16" above this line. This method works for any size cube and any size hole. (I've drawn the smaller cube so you can see how this works.)

6

Drill holes in the end-grain sides first. Then drill the other four faces. Always place the Xs in the same corner relative to the fence and stop-block.

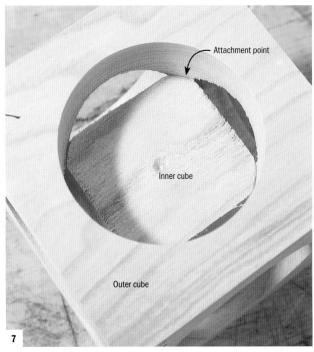

7

Drilling all six faces produces a cube in a cube. The inner cube is attached to the outer cube by a thin section of wood. The reason for drilling the end-grain faces first is to avoid breaking these weak attachment points. End-grain drilling requires more downward pressure than face-grain drilling.

8

Set the drill bit ¹⁄₃₂" deeper and repeat drilling all the holes. Again, drill the end-grain faces first. Use light pressure to avoid breaking the attachment points.

9

As you drill, check the thickness of the attachment points. Your goal is to make them as small as possible, to the point where the inner cube almost releases itself. This may require drilling some holes a tiny bit deeper. Draw check marks to show how many times you've drilled each hole.

10

Release the inner cube by cutting the attachment points with a thin knife, going with the grain. After cutting all eight corners, the inner cube will drop free. But it won't come out!

11

Sand the corners of the inner cube. Raise the inner cube above the outer cube by positioning the inner cube at a diagonal. Prop it up with a wedge or your fingers.

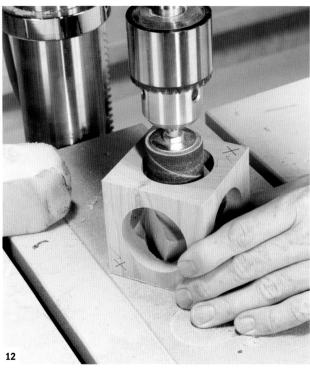

12

Sand burn marks or rough grain with a fine-grit drum-sanding attachment. Rub the drum with a crepe-rubber belt cleaner now and then to keep the drum working efficiently.

13

Smoothing the faces of the inner cube is tough, because they're hard to get to. I usually just leave them alone, but if you must do some clean-up work, use a file to start, then switch to sandpaper.

14

Dip the cube in oil to finish it. Rub thoroughly with a rag to remove the excess oil, and you're ready to play!

CHAPTER SIXTEEN
SCULPTED BALL

by Jock Holmen & Tom Caspar

People ask, "How in the world did you make that weird ball thing?"

The truth is, it's really quite simple: it's just a hollow cube with the corners cut off. Can you figure it out?

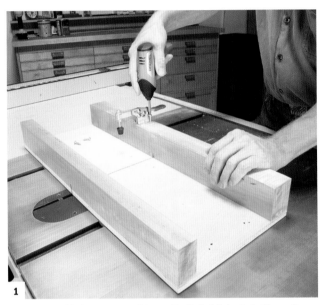

Precise cuts, safely done, are essential to making the ball. To begin, build a small crosscut sled with a fence wide enough to support a toggle clamp.

Fasten two pieces of ¼" tempered hardboard to the sled's bottom, centered over its slot. Butt the pieces together, then raise the blade and saw through the joint.

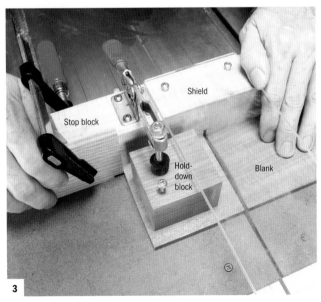

Saw twelve squares from two ¼" x 3½" x 24" blanks. Six are test pieces; the other six make one ball. Put a screw in the hold-down block as a fingerhold, to help you position the block. Add a plastic shield to deflect sawdust

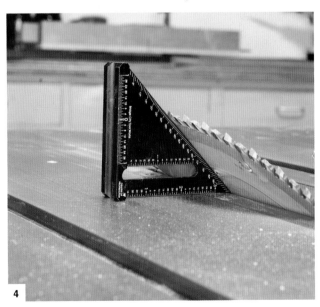

Remove the sled and tilt the blade to 45°. For the best results, use a 60-tooth crosscut blade for every cut on this project.

5 Remove both pieces of hardboard from the sled. Turn around the left piece and re-fasten it to the sled. Cut an angled slot all the way across it. Toss the waste piece.

6 On many contractor's saws, the blade moves out of square when it's tilted. Hold a piece against the blade and fence. Tape a shim to the fence if there's a gap at one corner. Ideally, you'd realign your saw to make it cut square, but this quick fix works well for this project.

7 Miter all four sides of a test piece. Start with an end-grain side, then turn it counter-clockwise as you go. Reposition the toggle clamp and plastic shield for these cuts. Just cut the square's edges; don't make it much smaller.

8 After the miter cuts, your piece must still be perfectly square. Adjust the shim, if necessary, to make the sides square, then cut four more test pieces.

9

Check the angle of the miters by holding the four test pieces together. You may have to adjust the blade's tilt to make these joints tight. Once you're set, miter all six "real" pieces.

10

Drill a 2⅛" diameter hole in the center of each piece using a Forstner bit. This jig locks the piece on three sides to ensure that it doesn't shift. Toggles keep your fingers out of the way.

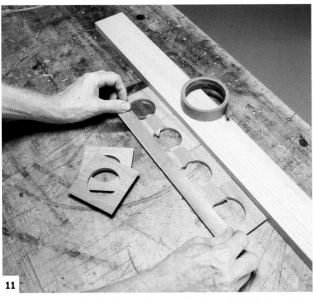

11

Tape four pieces together. Butt them against a straightedge to align their edges. Add the remaining two pieces to make a T.

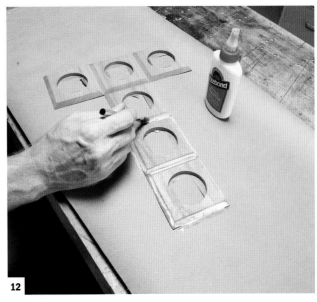

12

Turn over the assembly and spread glue on all the joints.

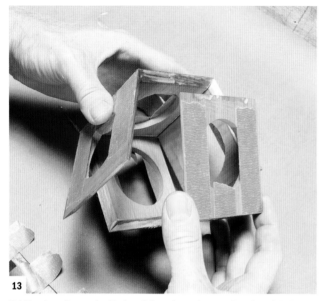

13

Fold the pieces into a cube. Put lots of short pieces of tape on the cube to hold the joints tight. Let the glue dry overnight, then remove the tape.

14

Add the righthand hardboard piece and two support boards to the sled. Support piece A is 1⅛" thick by 2⅛" wide; piece B is 1¾" thick by 2⅜" wide. Cut 45° miters on both pieces.

Centerline

15

Mark a centerline on the cube, then adjust the support boards side-to-side until the centerline falls exactly on the left isde of the sled's saw kerf. The cube should also fit tight against both support boards.

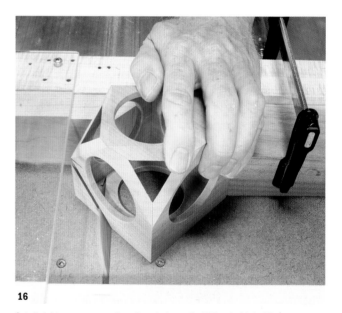

16

Cut all eight corners to transform the cube into a "ball." Set the blade ⅜" above the sled, then rotate the cube three times, making three cuts, to remove each corner. Finish the ball by dunking it in Danish oil and spraying it with lacquer.

CHAPTER SEVENTEEN

SPINNING TOP

by Alan Lacer

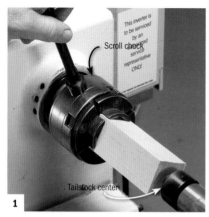

1 Use the tailstock center to hold the blank for the disc-shaped top bodies in position as you tighten the scroll chuck.

2 Round the blank with the spindle-roughing gouge.

3 Cut in with the narrow parting tool to establish the disc.

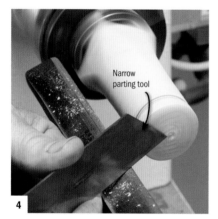

4 Exactly center a tiny recess in the disc's face.

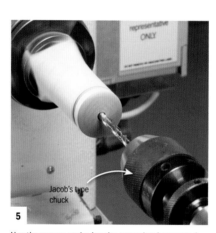

5 Use the recess and a Jacobs-type chuck mounted in the tailstock to drill a hole through the disc. This hole must be precisely centered for the top to spin without wobbling.

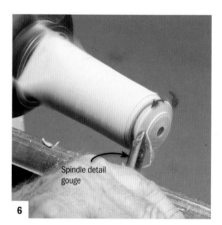

6 Shape the body as you would roll a bead. Start at the edge and cut toward the center, rotating the gouge as you go. When shaping the back, don't cut all the way to the center hole.

Most of us picture a spinning top as a simple wooden toy that stands upright when it spins. But in other parts of the world, the perception can be quite different. In Japan, for example, it is said that there are over one thousand different types and variations of tops.

I'm going to show you how to create one of those variations, a spinning top that's made out of two pieces of wood, instead of one. This miniature project offers a great opportunity to try your hand at precision turning. It also gives you the chance to add interest by using contrasting woods or even non-wood materials. And if one piece breaks, you can disassemble the top and install a replacement part.

Despite their diminutive size, you can make these tops on any lathe, and you only need four tools to create them – a spindle-roughing gouge (¾" to 1¼"), a narrow parting tool (³⁄₁₆" to ¼"), a ⅜" spindle-detail gouge and a skew chisel. If you are adept with your skew chisel, you can complete the entire project with it alone. You'll also need a ¼" drill bit and a Jacobs-type chuck that mounts into your tailstock (see Sources, page 101). Using a scroll-type chuck to hold the pieces is most convenient, but it's not necessary (see No-Frills Mounting, page 101 and Sources).

The wood you use is part of the design. Choose a hard, dense wood for the top's shaft, as both the spinning point and the finger-gripping area will be made from this material. Good choices for the shaft include hard maple, cherry, Osage orange, and numerous exotic woods such as ebony, bubinga, goncalo alves and blood-

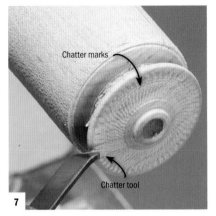

7 Create interesting texture with a chatter tool. A chatter tool's thin shaft is designed to vibrate when it contacts the wood, causing its tip to leave squiggly marks on the surface.

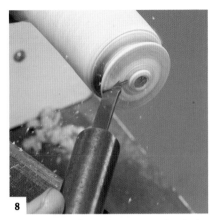

8 To chatter the top of the body, move the tool rest back and hold the chatter tool as shown. Start near the center and draw the tool toward the edge.

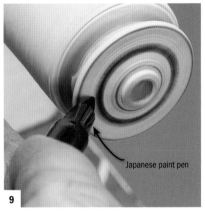

9 Accentuate chatter marks with color. Use a delicate touch to color only the high points, or flow the color into the crevices and then sand lightly, to remove the color from the high points.

10 Free the completed body by cutting in with the narrow parting tool. Catch the body in your hand or let it to fall onto a paper towel draped over the lathe's ways, and you're ready to go again.

11 To finish turning the body's bottom face, turn it around and remount it on a stub spindle that you've turned on a scrap block.

12 Complete the bottom face with light cuts and finish-sanding.

wood. Make sure this wood is well dried. For the top's disc-shaped body, you have many more options. Choose woods that contrast well in color or figure, again on the drier side. If you intend to chatter the body (I'll show this option), be sure and pick a very hard wood such as hard maple or one of the exotics mentioned above. To explore non-wood possibilities, consider materials such as solid surface composites, hard plastics, antler or even soft metals.

These tops operate by spinning them with your fingers, so they should be less than 1¾" in diameter. Most of the finger-spun tops that I make measure 1¼" to 1½". Also, you should plan to make these tops in multiples, because you can easily turn three to five of the disc-shaped bodies from a single blank.

TURN THE BODY

Cut a square blank of wood, approximately 4" long. Mark the center of one end of the blank.

Mount the block loosely in the scroll chuck, with the marked center towards the tailstock.

Engage the point of the tailstock center on your mark, to hold the blank perfectly centered while you tighten the chuck (**Photo 1**). Then back off the tailstock.

Round the blank using the spindle roughing gouge or your skew chisel (**Photo 2**).

Use the parting tool to establish the disc's thickness – usually between ¼" and ⅜" (**Photo 3**). Then mark the center of the disc's face (**Photo 4**).

Install a Jacobs-type chuck and drill a ¼" hole, precisely centered and about 1" deep (**Photo 5**).

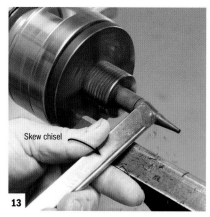

13 To create the top's shaft, start with a ½" square x 3" long blank mounted in the scroll chuck. Turn the blank round with the spindle roughing gouge or skew chisel. Then taper the end.

Skew chisel

14 Rough out the shoulder that will seat the top's body, the hub that it will mount on, and the gripping area for your fingers. Reduce this area to a diameter that's smaller than the hole in the top's body.

Shoulder

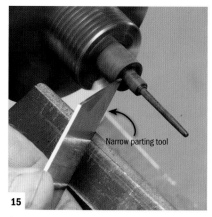

15 Create a cradle to seat the disc-shaped body by hollowing the shoulder with either the skew or a narrow parting tool.

Narrow parting tool

16 Here's the tricky part. Turn the hub's diameter to snugly fit the hole in the body—tight enough to hold the body on, but not so tight that you can't remove it. This step requires patience and lots of test fitting.

17 Shape the bottom like the outside of a tiny bowl, and create the spinning point as you part off the shaft. The spinning point's tip should be slightly rounded.

Skew chisel

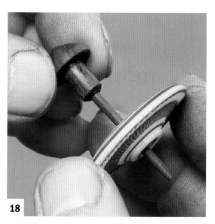

18 Press the body onto the shaft and give the top a spin.

Shape the body on both sides, using the spindle detail gouge (**Photo 6**). A slightly rounded body is more appealing than one that is cut straight in. Take care to cut the outside face cleanly. It will be the most visible part of the top. Finish-sand this face, unless you want to enhance it by adding chatter marks.

If you want to add chatter marks, you'll need a chatter tool (**Photo 7** and Sources). Learning to use this tool takes practice, so experiment on scrap materials, or plan to sacrifice a few top bodies as you get the hang of it. Here's a tip: a chatter tool makes a high-pitched noise when it's working properly. The lathe's speed, how hard you push, and how fast you draw the tool across the surface all effect the chatter pattern. (**Photo 8**).

Another option is to add rings of color, using Japanese paint pens, such as Tombow dual brush pens (**Photo 9** and Sources). Color adds interest to both chattered and smoothly sanded surfaces.

Part off the top body, either catching it in your hand or allowing it to fall into a paper towel (**Photo 10**).

Turn as many top bodies as the blank allows, until about 1" remains protruding from the chuck.

Using the narrow parting tool, turn a ¼" diameter spindle on a scrap block, so you can mount the bodies backwards, to finish the bottoms (**Photo 11**). This spindle should be slightly longer than the bodies' thickness. The goal is a fit that's snug enough to allow working the body, yet free enough to allow removing the body when it's done. Turning this spindle is actually great practice for an upcoming step – turning the hub that secures the body to the shaft. Finish the bottom face of each body to the same level as its top face (**Photo 12**).

TURN THE SHAFT

I turn the shafts one at a time. Start by mounting and truing a blank (**Photo 13**).

Rough out the shaft's components (**Photo 14**). I usually make the hub a bit longer than the body's thickness and the gripping area (for spinning the top) about 1¼" long. I like to make the gripping area pretty slender, but not less than ⅛" diameter. Finish-sand the gripping area.

Create a cradle to seat the body (**Photo 15**).

Size the hub (**Photo 16**).

Shape the bottom, but don't cut it off just yet (**Photo 17**). Finish-sand the bottom. Do not sand the hub, where the body mounts.

Use the skew chisel or the narrow parting tool to cut the shaft from the blank, leaving the bottom's spinning point slightly rounded.

Assemble the top (**Photo 18**). If the fit isn't quite tight enough, a small amount of glue will hold the two pieces together.

SOURCES

Packard Woodworks, www.packardwoodworks.com, (800) 683-8876, Oneway Talon Scroll Chuck #112670 $206.95 + #112606 $24.95 adapter for your lathe; Talon Spigot (small) Jaws #1122671 $40.95; Jacobs-Type Chuck #2MT, #111012 $36.95; KC Chatter Tool #105301 $49.95. ☺ Dick Blick, www. dickblick.com, (800) 828-4548, Tombow Brush Pens, set of 10 bright colors #21334-2219, $15.99. ⌀

No-Frills Mounting

Here's how to mount both blanks without using a scroll chuck. Shape the end of the blank for the top's body to a #2 Morse taper, so it fits snugly inside the drive shaft. Turn a concave shoulder on the blank, so it nests firmly against the driveshaft threads. Use the knockout bar for removal.

To mount the blank for the shaft, simply jam a ⁹/₁₆" square length into the driveshaft. You can chamfer the corners at the end, if you want, to make it easier to get started. Again, use the knockout bar for removal.

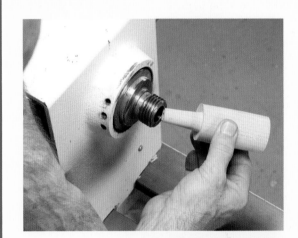

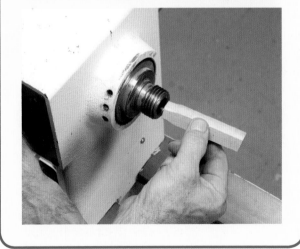

FUN FURNITURE

CHAPTER EIGHTEEN

PLAY TABLE

by Tom Caspar

1

Make a template from ¼" plywood or MDF. Draw the leg's inner curve by tracing around a coffee can. Tape sandpaper around the can and rotate it to make the template smooth.

2

Shape pieces of Baltic birch plywood, using the template and a router equipped with a top-bearing pattern bit, to make all four parts of the table. Use the same template for each leg.

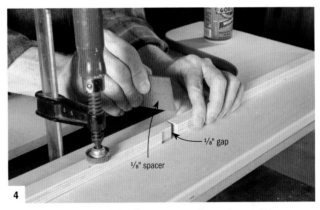

3

Saw dados down the length of the table's sides and ends. These dados will receive the ledger strips that support the table's platform.

4

Glue the ledger strips in the dados. Use spacers to make sure there are ⅛" gaps between the three ledgers on the table's long sides.

Back when I was a kid, one of my favorite pastimes was playing with a Brio wooden train set. I spread the tracks all over the living room floor, much to the consternation of a very tolerant mom.

Now that I'm the grandfather of a 3-year-old who also loves wooden trains – especially Thomas the Tank Engine – I've built a play table based on a Brio design. It reigns in the play area and allows my grandson to stand, and me to kneel, while indulging our train fantasies. Of course, the table can also be used for Legos or blocks or anything kids like to build up and knock down – its high sides prevent loose pieces from scattering all over the house.

I've designed the table to be easy to put together and take apart. All of the pieces form a neat bundle for storing in a closet or shipping to kids who live far away.

The best material for making the table is ¾" Baltic birch plywood. Having thick outer plies and no voids, it's extremely durable. Baltic birch comes in 5x5 sheets; other similar multi-ply products that would do just as well come in 4x8 sheets. To build the table, you'll need one 5x5 sheet or half of a 4x8 sheet.

Before you cut into the plywood, make a template for one of the table's legs (**Fig. B**). Use ¼" MDF, hardboard or plywood – MDF is best because it's very easy to shape and sand smooth. Make the template at least 30" long, so it will overlap the center of the table's longest sides. Cut the template's straight sections on the table saw to ensure that they're square. Cut the curved portions using a jigsaw or bandsaw, then sand them to remove any lumps or divots (**Photo 1**).

Use the template to lay out the table's sides (A) and ends (B) on your plywood (**Fig. E**). Cut the plywood into two 24" x 48" pieces so they're easy to manage, then cut out the ends and sides. Stay about 1/16" to ⅛" away from any line that you can't saw accurately or easily on the table saw, so the pieces are oversize. I used a jigsaw at first, but the plywood tore out quite a lot. I got better results with a bandsaw and a ¼" blade.

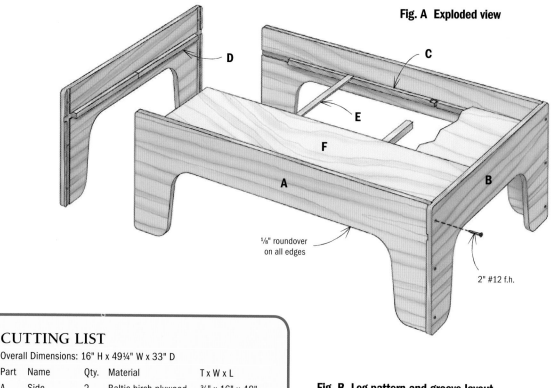

Fig. A Exploded view

⅛" roundover
on all edges

2" #12 f.h.

CUTTING LIST
Overall Dimensions: 16" H x 49¼" W x 33" D

Part	Name	Qty.	Material	T x W x L
A	Side	2	Baltic birch plywood	¾" x 16" x 48"
B	End	2	Baltic birch plywood	¾" x 16" x 33"
C	Side ledger	6	Baltic birch plywood	¾" x ¾" x 15⅝"
D	End ledger	4	Baltic birch plywood	¾" x ¾" x 14½"
E	Brace	2	Steel angle iron	1" x 1" x 30⅝"
F	Platform	2	MDF	½" x 15⁵⁄₁₆" x 47¾"

Fig. B Leg pattern and groove layout

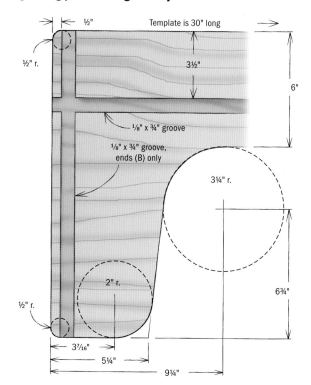

½"

Template is 30" long

½" r.

3½"

6"

⅛" x ¾" groove

⅛" x ¾" groove,
ends (B) only

3¼" r.

6¾"

½" r.

2" r.

½" r.

3⁷⁄₁₆"

5¼"

9¼"

Clamp the template to each piece and use it as a guide for your router, using a top-bearing pattern bit (**Photo 2**). When you're done with all the pieces, use a ⅛" roundover bit with a bearing to soften every exposed edge.

Next, set up a dado set to make a groove that fits the plywood's thickness. Your plywood will probably be a little less than ¾" thick, so you'll have to use shims to make a groove that's the correct width. Cut ⅛" deep grooves down the length of all four side and end pieces (**Photo 3**). Cut vertical grooves down both legs of the end pieces—but not the side pieces. All of these grooves help align the parts when you assemble the table.

Cut ledger strips (C and D) to fit into the grooves. Using the dado set, cut notches on both ends of two side ledgers (**Fig. D**). Glue the ledgers into the grooves (**Photo 4**). On the side pieces, start with the middle ledgers and make sure they're centered. Use a ⅛" spacer to position the outer ledgers.

5

Drill holes for the screws that will hold the table together. Using this jig ensures that the holes will be plumb and in the right spot.

6

Fasten the table together. Place the second end piece on top of the sides to hold the table square. The end pieces have dados that lock the side pieces in position.

7

Install steel angle iron in the gaps between the ledger pieces. The rigidity of the angle iron prevents the platform from sagging.

Fig. C Drilling jig

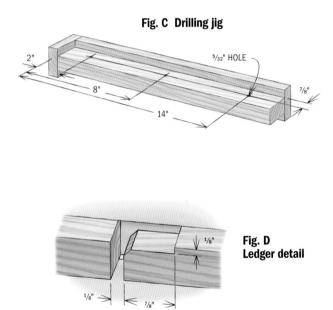

2"

8"

14"

⁵⁄₃₂" HOLE

⅞"

**Fig. D
Ledger detail**

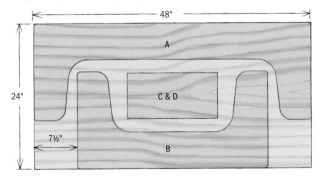

⅛"

⅛"

⅞"

Drill holes through the end pieces for the screws that will fasten the table together (**Photo 5**). I built a reversible jig for this job (**Fig. C**), but it's not strictly necessary. Clamp the table together, making sure it's square, and drill pilot holes into the side pieces (**Photo 6**). Install the screws.

Measure the distance between the side rails, then cut pieces of steel angle iron (E) to fit. Drop the angle iron in the notches between the ledgers (**Photo 7**). The angle iron makes the table sturdy enough for a kid to stand on, should playtime get really out of hand!

Cut the platform (F) to fit. I made the platform from two pieces of ½" MDF and connected the pieces with five biscuits – glued in only one piece – so the two halves would stay aligned. These pieces are no wider than the table's ends and sides, so they store compactly. You could also use ¼" hardboard for the platform, but it should be one big piece because it's too thin to align with biscuits. Take the table apart and finish it with three coats of poly.

Fig. E Plywood cutting diagram

48"

24"

A

C & D

B

7½"

CHAPTER NINETEEN

TRACTOR TRAILER TOYBOX

by Alan Krogh

After designing and building toy boxes and doll furniture for four granddaughters, I wanted to come up with something suitable for a grandson should we ever be blessed with one. This is a multifunctional project – a lot of fun to build and play with (with or without a grandchild) as well as a perfect storage box for miscellaneous cargo.

This mobile toy storage tractor-trailer truck features a hood that opens up for tune-up work on the V8 engine. Driver- and passenger-side doors have latches to keep them shut during transport time. The cab seat is upholstered, as well as the interior of the cab. By lifting up on the brass air horns, the roof of the sleeper opens up for additional storage.

The trailer can be detached and left standing full of toys or other cargo by flipping down the parking dolly. The lid is attached with a piano hinge and features a toy box lid support.

The rig is constructed with ¾" and ½" ash and a ½" x 4' x 4' sheet of birch-face plywood. Inlaid walnut veneer is used for the sleeper windows and trailer decoration. Walnut is also used for the front and back bumpers.

WORKING FROM THE GROUND UP

Completing the chassis and wheels first is helpful during the final assembly of the cab and hood portions of the rig.

Cut the tractor chassis sides, spreaders and end cap to size, then use a ¾" Forstner bit to drill the axle holes. Apply glue to the mating surfaces and assemble the chassis with two screws per joint.

TRAILER CHASSIS

Assemble the trailer's chassis using the same simple butt joints, glue and screws.

Use two self-closing overlay hinges for the parking dolly. Mount the hinges to the back of the front spreader, orienting them so they snap to attention when down. I used a scrap of ash for the cross piece. Two lengths of bead chain limit the swing of the dolly to 90°.

TIRES & WHEELS

All of the tires are 3½" in diameter. The two front tires are made from one-by pine; two-by stock provides the necessary traction for the eight dual tires. Rounding out the bill of material, I used ⅛" ash for the 2⅛"-diameter hub/rims.

Before cutting the dual tires, drill a 1⅛"-diameter hole at the center point to a depth of ½". The stopped hole creates the illusion of a dual tire and makes room for the hubcap.

Change to a ¾" bit and drill through the rest of the way. Drill the axle holes in the one-by pieces using the ¾" bit.

Mount the two hinges to the front frame, orienting so the hinge snaps shut in the closed, or upright position. I used a scrap of ash, ⅜" x ⅜" left over from making the trailer corner mouldings, for the cross piece.

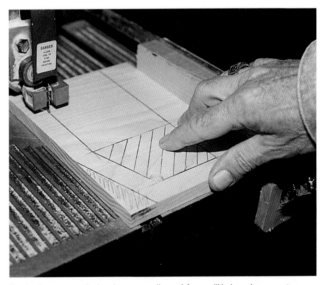

Cut the doors out on the band saw or scroll saw. A fence will help make your cuts more accurate. Keep the inside piece because you'll use it again when making the doors that open and close.

The wheel rims are made the same way with a few added steps. Begin by drawing a 1¾"-diameter circle on the ⅛" stock. Divide it into eight equal parts. These points are where the wheel lugs (escutcheon pins) will be installed.

Drill out the axle opening using the ¾" bit for the two front rims and 1⅛" for the eight dual tires.

Although I used a circle-cutting jig to make the wheel and rim cutouts, a good eye, steady hands and a band saw can make

TRACTOR-TRAILER TOY BOX

No.	Item	T	W	L	Material	Notes
		Dimensions (inches)				
TRACTOR CHASSIS FRAME						
2	Sides (A)	¾	2	22¼	Ply	
2	Spreaders (B)	¾	2	6½	Ply	
1	End cap (C)	¾	2	8	Ply	
1	Front axle	¾ dia		9¾	Dowel	
2	Rear axles	¾ dia		10⅜	Dowel	
TRAILER CHASSIS FRAME						
2	Sides (D)	¾	3	27	Ply	
3	Spreaders (E)	¾	3	6½	Ply	
1	End cap (F)	¾	3	8	Ply	
2	Rear axles	¾ dia		10⅜	Dowel	
TIRES AND WHEELS						
2	Front tires	¾	3½ dia.		Pine	
8	Dual tires	1½	3½ dia.		Pine	
10	Tire rims	⅛	2⅛ dia.		Ash	
10	Hubcaps	1 dia.	wooden balls			cut in half
TRACTOR CAB						
1	Cab floor (G)	½	9	8½	Birch ply	
1	Firewall (H)	½	8	5	Birch ply	
1	Sleeper back (I)	½	9	10¼	Birch ply	
2	Cab sides (J)	½	5½	8	Ash	
1	Cab top (K)	½	5½	8	Ash	
2	Sleeper sides (L)	½	4½	11	Ash	
1	Sleeper frt (M)	½	2¾	9	Ash	cut to fit
1	Sleeper top (N)	½	3¼	9	Ash	cut to fit
2	Fuel tanks (O)	1	1½	11½	Ash	
4	Window inlay	Veneer	1	Various	Walnut	
1	Hitch pltfrm (P)	¾	8	8½	Ash	
1	Hitch (Q)	1⅛ dia.		1½	Dowel	
2	Exhaust stacks	½ dia.		13	Walnut dowel	
1	Seat bench (R)	¾	7½	2½	Ply	
1	Upholstery		9	8¾	Vinyl	
1	Seat back (S)	⅜	7½	4	Ply	
1	Upholstery		9½	5½	Vinyl	
1	Seat riser (T)	¾	1¾	6	Ply	cut to fit
1	Steering whl	2½ dia.			Hardwood	
1	Dashboard (U)	¾	¾	8	Ash	
1	Front bmpr (V)	⅜	2¾	9	Walnut	
ENGINE COMPARTMENT & FRONT FENDERS						
2	Frt fenders (W)	1⅜	2½	5½	Ash	
1	Grill (X)	½	3½	5¼	Ash	
1	Hood top (Y)	½	5¼	5¼	Ash	cut long to fit later
2	Hood sides (Z)	½	5	5¼	Ash	
2	Headlights (AA)	¾ dia.		3/16	Dowel	
TRAILER						
2	Sides (BB)	½	12	36	Ply	
2	Ends (CC)	½	12	12	Ply	
1	Bot (DD)	½	11½	35	Ply	
4	Corner trim (EE)	¾	¾	12⅛	Ash	
2	Side decoration	⅛	¾	36	Ash	cut to fit
2	End decoration	⅛	¾	12	Ash	cut to fit
2	Stripes		½	36	Walnut veneer	
2	Stripes		¼	36	Walnut veneer	
2	Top banding	⅛	½	12	Ash	
1	Top banding	⅛	½	36	Ash	
TRAILER LID						
1	Center (FF)	½	8¾	32¼	Ply	
2	Edges (GG)	¾	2	36¼	Ash	
2	Ends (HH)	¾	2	8¾	Ash	

HARDWARE LIST

11/16" x 60" piano hinge

1	toy box lid support
1	pkg solid brass knobs for air horns
1	pkg ⅜" overlay hinges
1	2" bead chain for trailer dolly
10	1" hardwood balls
1	2½" wheel for steering wheel
2	5/16" bullet catches

for smooth-riding wheels. Breaking the edge between the sidewalls and tread area gives the tires a more realistic appearance.

The frames and tires are the only parts that are stained. It is easier to do so prior to assembly. I used a brown dye for coloring the frames, tires and steering wheel. Stain the rims yellow.

HUBCAPS

While the economy associated with splitting five, 1" wooden balls in half to make 10 hubcaps appealed to my woodworker frugality, I decided to spring for 10 balls (about $3) and keep all my fingers. Using a large countersink chucked into your drill press, make 10 equal-depth divots along a length of one-by pine. After gluing the balls in the depressions, grain horizontal, switch to a #6 countersink bit and predrill the screw holes at the top centers of the balls for mounting the hubcaps to the axles. Finally, guided by a fence on your band saw, turn the mounting board on edge and lop off half spheres like bologna through a slicer.

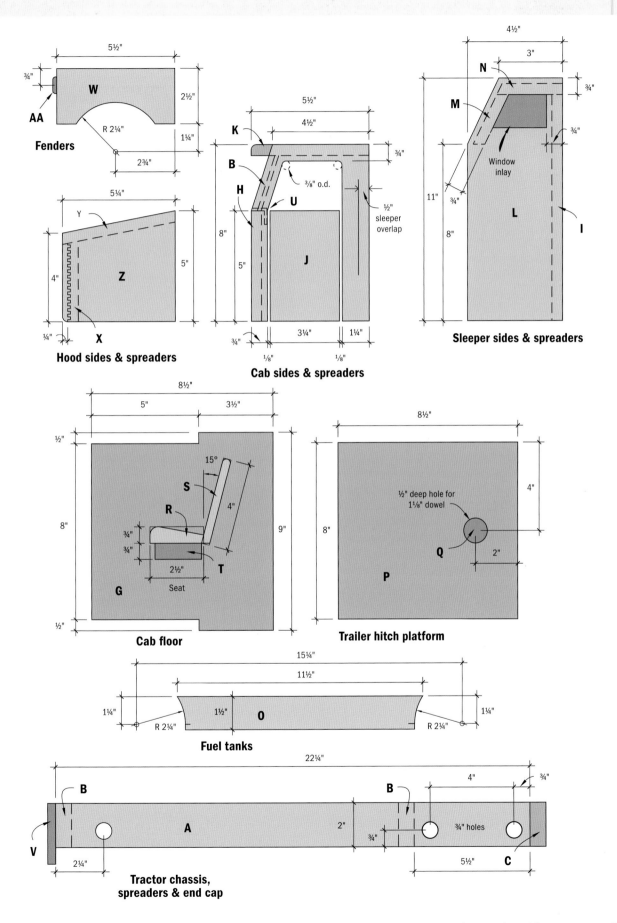

Fenders

W

AA

5½"

¾"

2½"

1¼"

R 2¼"

2¾"

Hood sides & spreaders

Y

Z

X

5¼"

4"

5"

¼"

Cab sides & spreaders

K

B

H

U

J

5½"

4½"

¾"

⅜" o.d.

½" sleeper overlap

8"

5"

¾"

3¼"

1¼"

⅛"

⅛"

Sleeper sides & spreaders

N

M

L

I

4½"

3"

¾"

¾"

Window inlay

11"

¾"

8"

Cab floor

G

S

R

T

Seat

8½"

5"

3½"

½"

8"

½"

15°

4"

¾"

¾"

2½"

9"

Trailer hitch platform

P

Q

8½"

½" deep hole for 1⅛" dowel

4"

8"

2"

Fuel tanks

O

15¼"

11½"

1¼"

1½"

1¼"

R 2¼"

R 2¼"

Tractor chassis, spreaders & end cap

B

A

B

C

V

22¼"

4"

¾"

2"

¾"

¾" holes

2¼"

5½"

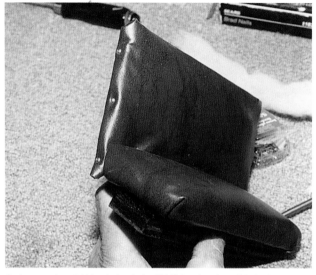

On the seat edges, fold the vinyl under itself. Affix it to the edges of the back using three or four escutcheon pins as shown below. Mount the seat riser block to the bottom of the seat bench.

Here you can see how the cab goes together. The sleeper roof will be constructed after the cab roof is installed. And the cab doors will be made and installed after the cab, seat and upholstery installation is complete.

TRACTOR CAB

Refer to the drawings on the previous page and the cutting list for the cab parts.

Note that the driver's seat, steering wheel and interior upholstering must be installed prior to attaching the roof.

Each cab side and door is made from one piece of 8" x 5½" wood. I used a band saw to make the cuts, drilling ⅜" holes in the upper corners of the doors to aid in negotiating the corners. Set the doors aside after marking their original orientation.

SLEEPER SIDES

Cut out the sides, ease all edges except the bottom, and inlay the walnut veneer windows. I used 1³⁄₁₆"-wide edging veneer for this. After cutting the windows from the banding, trace the shapes onto the sides of the sleeper and remove enough stock to accomplish a flush inlay.

TRAILER HITCH PLATFORM

Cut the trailer hitch platform to the 8" x 8½" dimensions. Again, use your roundover bit on the top back and sides of the plate, leaving the front edge straight to mount flush with the cab back. Using a 1⅛" Forstner bit, drill ½" into the plate, 2" in from the back. Make sure not to drill completely through the plate. Leave ¼" for hitch mounting purposes.

Round over the top edge of a 1⅛" hardwood dowel. Cut a 1½" length and mount it in the plate using glue and a screw driven through the bottom of the platform.

CAB SEAT

See the drawings for a cross section through the seat, seat back and riser. First round the ends of the seat and back. I can staple far better than I can sew, so I used a staple gun to attach the upholstery. After laying a bit of padding on the seat bench, wrap the vinyl around and staple to the bottom of the seat, leaving room in the center of the bottom for the riser block.

Now lay a bit of padding on the front of the seat back, staple one edge to the bottom, and wrap the vinyl over the top and back to the bottom and staple. On the edges, fold the vinyl under itself. Use three or four escutcheon pins to tack the edges.

CAB ASSEMBLY

The firewall, cab sides, sleeper sides and sleeper back mount to the edges of the cab floor. After dry-fitting to ensure tight joints, glue and nail the joints using 1" brads. Note that the front edges of the sleeper overlap the back of the cab sides by ½". The sleeper roof is constructed after the cab roof is installed. The cab doors are hung after the seat and steering wheel are installed.

ENGINE COMPARTMENT & FENDERS

Cut the hood top, sides and grill to size. I used the table saw to make the grill bars. Lower the blade to ⅛" and install a zero-clearance insert. Set the fence ¼" from the blade. Using a push stick and featherboard, slide the grill stock through the saw. Move the fence another ¼" from the blade and make another pass.

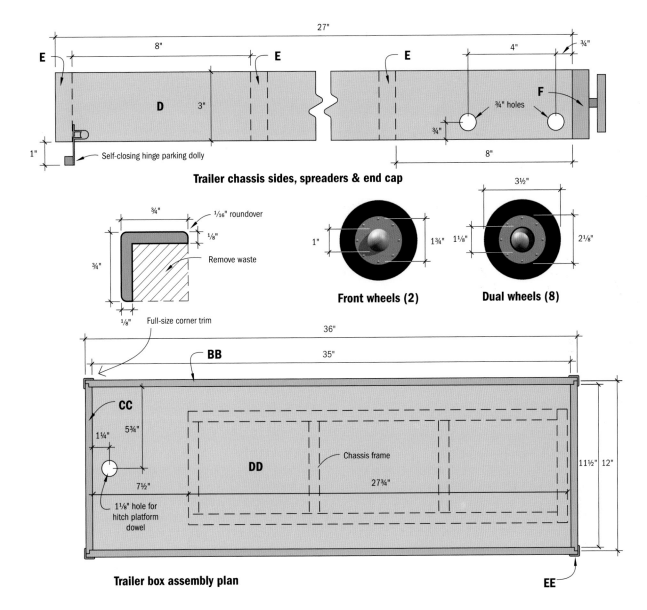

Trailer chassis sides, spreaders & end cap

Front wheels (2)

Dual wheels (8)

Trailer box assembly plan

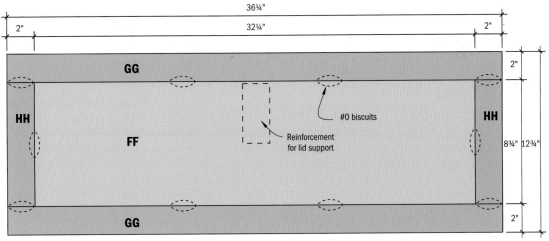

Trailer lid assembly plan

Prior to final installation, carpet the interior of the roof. I started the carpet where the top of the windshield meets the roof, about ¾" back from the leading edge.

The lid is a simple frame-and-panel assembled with biscuits and glue. But because the panel is a piece of plywood, you don't need to worry about seasonal expansion or contraction.

This will result in a ⅛" groove and ⅛" raised portion. Keep moving the fence in ¼" increments until you have completed the grill.

Assemble the top, sides and grill per the drawings. The hood top edges should extend beyond the front and rear of the hood sides to allow for final trimming.

After you've cut the fenders to size, install short slices of rounded ¾" dowel for the headlights.

To keep things rolling along, install a length of ¾" dowel, about 18", through the front axle hole on the cab frame. Set the assembled cab and hood portions in position on the frame and mount the fenders to the hood sides, using glue and screws driven from the engine compartment.

After aligning the face of the grill with the front of the cab chassis, mount the hood to the frame with a piano hinge. The ¼" radius at the bottom of the hood sides allow full opening of the hood assembly when the front bumper is installed.

Install the front bumper to the front of the frame using glue and escutcheon pins.

ENGINE INSTALLATION

The engine is made from a 2½" x 3¾" piece of pine with a bevel, at about 30°, for the valve covers on each side. I made the valve covers from two pieces of ¾" walnut, 1⅛" wide. The motor is installed by fastening a short piece of walnut to an oil pan and then to the bottom of the cab.

FUEL TANKS & DETAILS

The tanks should fit flush with the sides of the sleeper. They're mounted to the frame with two screws driven from the inside of the frame.

The exhaust stacks (to be installed at the discretion of the builder) mount to the back of the sleeper sides. To secure them, I used 1", 18-gauge brads.

After a brief snooze at the rest stop, place the cab seat in the appropriate position on the cab floor and draw a line around the seat base. Remove the seat and drill two clearance holes, within the seat base rectangle, through the floor.

I used a short length of carpet runner for the cab upholstery. Cut a length (about 24") 8" wide for the firewall/cab portion and 9" for the sleeper area. I used a stapler to mount the carpet and turned to my hot glue gun for the difficult-to-reach areas.

Be sure to leave a ½" area uncarpeted on the top and front edge of the sleeper sides for the sleeper lid installation. Install the seat by placing it into position and driving two screws up through the base.

The steering wheel is a spoked wheel sold for making toy cars. Using the axle of the wheel as the steering column will allow your youngster to negotiate tight turns.

The dashboard is an extra length of corner molding from the trailer. Mount it on the inside of the cab over the firewall carpeting. Some trimming may be needed if it intrudes into the engine compartment. Drill an angled hole into the dashboard for the steering wheel column; press and glue into place.

Now carpet the interior of the roof and install it. The sleeper cab lid is made from a 6" x 9" piece of ½" ash. Tilt the saw to 26.5°, 3" from the fence, and rip it to form the sleeper top and front. Install the front-facing windows following the same technique used for the side windows.

Mount the assembled lid to the top of the sleeper back using a 9" length of piano hinge.

The use of jewelry box pulls for the air horns gives a bit of flair to the rig. Because of the angle of the front piece, I drilled an angled cavity to enable the air horns to be mounted perpendicular to the cab roof.

DOORS & WHEELS

The doors need ⅛" clearance on each of the edges for hinge and door latch installations. They are mounted to the sides with 5" lengths of ½"-wide piano hinge. After hanging the doors, install bullet catches to keep the doors closed.

After drilling pilot holes in the ends of the axles, slide the axles into the mounting locations, place the tires in position and install the hubcaps using one screw through the hubcap into the axle ends.

TRAILER

The box is constructed from plywood joined at the corners with rabbet joints. After cutting the plywood for the box carcase, make a ¼" rabbet on the joining edges of the sides and ends.

To dress up the trailer, I inlaid a little walnut on the sides. The top strip is 4¼" from the bottom of the box, and the lower is 3¼". Cut the recess using a dado stack or router. I used an 8' length of 1³⁄₁₆" walnut edge banding. Glue the strips into the slots and sand the sides.

Drill a 1⅛" hole through the box bottom to accept the tractor-trailer hitch. Use a backer board on the backside of the hole to reduce tear-out.

Assemble the sides, ends and bottom with glue and brads (the bottom slips inside the sides). The seams will be covered by the corner and bottom pieces.

The box corners are made from ¾" x ¾" ash. Round the edges using a roundover bit on the router table. Set the fence on the table saw ⅛" from the blade and ⅝" high. Run the strip through, reorient the strip and make another pass, removing the center portion of the strip. Since you cannot use the blade guard during this, great care must be taken. Fingerboards and push sticks are a must.

This will leave an outside ⅛" corner piece, rounded on three sides. Cut into four 12⅛" strips. The extra ⅛" of length is needed for the edge banding space on three of the top edges as well as a dado for the piano hinge, making the lid fit flush on the box.

Rip ¾" stock into ⅛" thickness – two 36" and two 12" lengths. Rip the ½" ash stock into ⅛" thickness – one at 36" and two 12" lengths.

With glue and brads, mount the ½" stock on the top edges of the box, leaving one long side without the edge banding. This side is where the piano hinge goes.

Install the bottom ¾" decoration pieces around the bottom of the box.

Turn the box upside down and lay the chassis in place. The rear of the chassis should be 1" from the rear of the box. Trace its outline and set it aside. Drill pilot holes within the outline through the bottom, glue and clamp the chassis in place and turn the unit over and fasten the frame and box together with countersunk screws driven from the inside of the box.

The lid of the box is made from plywood with a ¾"-thick frame biscuited to the plywood center panel, and is mounted with a piano hinge. Round over the frame pieces, then attach them to the center panel using biscuits and glue.

After the glue has cured, sand the top and bottom of the lid. Round the outside corners and use a roundover bit in the router to relieve the outside edges.

Mount the lid to the box with a piano hinge and toy box support. Because of the ½" thickness of the plywood, I reinforced the mounting locations on the top and side with ¼" hardwood scraps.

Install the axles, wheels and hubcaps. Mount the back bumper (a ⅜" x 2½" x 11⅜" piece) using screws. I used the inside cutouts of the corner mouldings as spacers between the frame and back bumper.

FINISHING

Two coats of 50/50 cut white shellac brings out the grain of the ash. I like the protection and ease of application of General Finishes Arm-R-Seal for these types of projects. Two top coats of this oil and urethane top coat gives the rig some protection and a just-waxed appearance.

Take the rig out for a test drive – diesel motor and air brake noises are optional. Happy motoring! Keep on truckin' and woodworkin'!

Tire Making 101

Use a scrap of wood large enough to cover the band saw table slot and saw blade kerf path, about 5" x 7". On the bottom, attach a wood strip about 8" long to serve as a slot insert guide. Draw a line, at a right angle to the saw blade kerf, on the top of the jig. Start the saw and slide the jig slowly into the blade. When the saw blade meets the perpendicular line, turn off the saw. Carefully place a "stop-block" in the slot behind the slot insert and clamp in place. This will serve as the starting point for cutting out the tires. Back the jig out and measure 1¾" from the saw blade kerf, along the line drawn on the jig. This will be the axis point for the 3½"-diameter tires. Cut a short piece of ¾" dowel and mount it vertically on that center point, making sure that the dowel is square with the jig face. The tire block should rotate easily on this dowel. If it doesn't, apply some wax or lightly sand the dowel

To actually make the tires, place one of the tire blocks on the dowel and hold the block firmly while sliding the jig toward the saw blade. When the jig meets the stop-block, hold the jig securely in place and rotate the tire block clockwise until the circle is complete. Turn the saw off and back the jig out through the entrance kerf.

Some sanding of the tread area may be needed. I used a dowel to act as an axle and a belt sander, mounted upside down, to smooth down the cut marks. Breaking the edge between the sidewalls and tread area also give the tire a more realistic appearance. After final sanding, stain the tires.

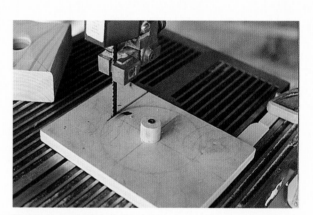

Place the tire-making jig on the band saw.

Then it's a simple matter of slowly rotating the stock to create a tire that needs just a little sanding.

CHAPTER TWENTY
PIRATE CHEST

by Megan Fitzpatrick

Don't let the curved top of this pirate chest scare you. It's a lot less tricky than it may appear – and it's excellent practice with your block plane.

For this build, you'll have to venture a bit beyond the home center – but stop there to pick up a 6' 1x12, two 8' 1x8s and 21' of 1½" by 1 slats (though if you have a table saw or band saw with which to rip the slats, that will be more economical). Also get 40 or so upholstery nails, a box of at least 40 6d masonry nails, a hasp, two 4" gate hinges and two handles. Go for the cheap zinc-coated hardware; I'll give you a few options for aging it. Now you need to visit a "big and tall" clothing department for some 50" (or better, 60") leather belts. At 50" (the largest available where I shopped), I had to cut the belts and nail them at the front and back edge of the bottom. Just 10 additional inches would have meant no cuts – the belts would have wrapped all the way around (and saved a little time and trouble).

BUILD THE BOX FIRST

To make things simple, I used the full width of my stock lumber for the front, back and sides. So I set up a stop at the miter saw and cut the four front and back pieces from the 1x8s to 22" long. Then, I cut the two sides to 14" long – but, because dimensional lumber can vary slightly in width, you should butt the two front pieces (or the two back pieces) against one another, and cut the length of your side pieces to match that measurement.

In other words, it's always risky to rely on the cutlist or drawing for exact dimensions; yours could end being slightly different in any build. Always generate measurements from the actual parts when possible.

Both the front and back have chamfers on the long edges where the two pieces meet in the middle, which serve two purposes: They create a shadow line for a more pleasing aesthetic, and they hide the fact that the two pieces don't form a perfect joint (an impossibility with two home center edges). I simply eyeballed the chamfers using a block plane held at a 45° (or so) angle for each piece, and continued planing until I was content with the chamfer depth. If eyeballing it isn't your style, measure and mark a line across both the face and edge at ⅛" and plane down to your lines.

Now clamp the front and back pieces in place to the sides, then decide on your nail layout (I used on three nails on each plank end: one ¾" from each edge and one in the middle) and drill ⅛" pilot holes – which seems big, but it isn't. In fact, the wood may still split when you sink the nail – especially if you aren't careful to line it the wide part of the nail in line with the grain. (If you get a split, don't panic. Just pull the nail out and drill a bigger pilot hole.) Masonry nails, like period cut nails, are actually wedges, so if you align them incorrectly, you're basically wedging the wood apart – especially in this case, when you're nailing so close to the end.

No wedgies. When using masonry nails (or period cut nails) it's important to align the wedge-shaped nail so that the wide part is going with the grain in the top piece of wood. If you align it across the grain, you'll likely wedge the grain right open and cause a split.

No matter which approach you choose to fit the slats for the curved top, you'll need to plane angles on the slat edges with your block plane to get the pieces to fit.

With the case assembled, cut the bottom to length just a hair undersized at the miter saw, then take a few strokes along a long edge with your block plane. The piece should be a tight fit in the bottom of the case. I knocked it in with a rubber mallet, then put everything on the floor to push the bottom piece firmly in place. Measure, mark and drill pilot holes. I used five nails across the front and back, and three on either side. Locate the side nails in far enough that you won't hit the ones coming in from the front and back.

Do you really need such big nails to hold this small box together? Of course not. And do you really need to use so many of them? Again, no. But the large heads and interesting shape add to the overall look of the chest. It's all about the aesthetics.

MAKE A CURVED TOP

First, use a compass to mark the two side pieces for the top with a 5¹⁵⁄₁₆" radius – or just use a 5-gallon bucket to trace the curve. Either way, the apex of the curve is 4" from the bottom center of the pieces.

Before you start attaching the slats to your top end pieces, you'll first have to plane an angle on at least one long edge of each slat (and on both edges as you round the top). What angle? Well, I eyeballed it. I held my first slat in position at the bottom front edge, and marked an angle on the end that looked as if, once the waste was removed, it would allow the slat edge to sit flat to the top edge of the case. Then I marked the cut along the edges of the slat,

clamped it into position, and used a block plane to plane down to my lines.

I temporarily secured the slat in position to the top end pieces with one 2d finish nail at each end, then fit the next slat in the same manner, marking the angle on the edge facing the previous slat while leaving the top edge at 90°, until I came to the two center top pieces. Those must be planed along both long edges. Then I worked down the other side, with the angle planed on the side facing the back edge of the chest. (Or you can mark and plane angles on both edges of each piece for a tighter fit, as shown in the drawing.)

Once all the slats are fit and temporarily tacked in place, drill pilot holes for 4d finish nails, mark the order in which each slat is attached to the ends, then pull the slats off. Now apply glue to each long edge as you reattach the slats in order using 4d finish nails. Use a nail set to set each nail well below the wood's surface (and using an oversized nail set will help you jump-start the "aging" process, by making a bigger indentation, giving the top the appearance of long use and abuse).

Once the glue dries, use your block plane to smooth the arris where each slat meets (double-check first that all your 4d nails are below the surface; if they're not, you'll nick your plane blade).

I painted my piece dark brown, then beat the heck out of it using a bunch of keys and a hammer. This process exposed raw wood in the wounds, but I added a topcoat of dark Briwax paste wax to simulate years of dirt, working it in well to the newly exposed wood.

To age your hardware, you have a few options. You can soak everything in vinegar to remove the bright coating, or simply paint it black. Or grab a propane torch and burn the finish off (make sure you do this in a well-ventilated area and have a bucket of water on hand for quenching).

Attach the hardware, then wrap the belts around the chest, buckle them, drive in a bunch of upholstery nails to effect a studded look (I used them every 1½" across the top, and every 2" on the front and back). If your belt is less than 60" long, you'll have to cut it and attach it at the top and bottom edge – I suggest long staples for this, covered with a upholstery nail.

Now load your chest with booty and start talking like a pirate.

CUTTING LIST

NO.	PART	STOCK	DIMENSIONS (T, W, L)	
			INCHES	MILLIMETERS
4	Front/back planks	Pine	¾ × 7 × 22	19 × 178 × 559
2	Case sides	Pine	¾ × 11¼ × 14	19 × 285 × 356
1	Bottom	Pine	¾ × 11¼ × 20½	19 × 285 × 521
2	Top sides	Pine	¾ × 11¼ × 4	19 × 285 × 102
12	Top slats	Pine	¾ × 1½ × 22	19 × 38 × 559

3-D View

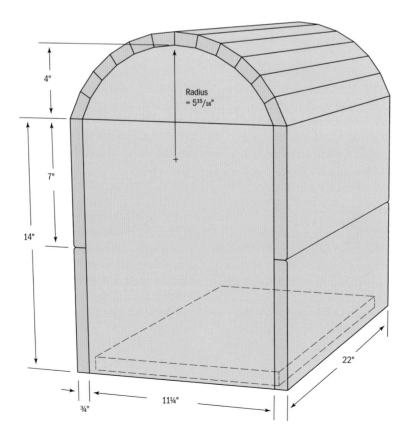

4"

7"

14"

Radius = 5¹⁵/₁₆"

22"

11¼"

¾"

CHAPTER TWENTY-ONE

STEP STOOL

by Glen D. Huey

A thin strip of wood makes the perfect tool for designing a curve.

You may not remember when you looked up at the sink, or when you climbed up to the potty – but if you'd had a few extra inches on your legs, things would have been so much easier. This stool can do that for youngsters – and help you clean out your scrap bin too.

A project like this generally begins with a trip to buy lumber, but you probably have the needed material – scraps – floating around your shop. This especially holds true if you paint this piece instead of go all wack-nutty with figured maple like I did. But if you need wood, simply head off to the store with your cut sheet in hand.

On this project, you can cut the pieces to size at the beginning of the build (most times it's better to cut to length and width as you need the parts in case things change). Once the parts are cut, the majority of the work is on the sides; they get laid out, drilled and shaped.

Find and mark the locations for the holes prior to any shaping work and make sure you have mirrored layout images. Keeping the drill square to the workpiece, bore the two ¾"-diameter holes and one ¼"-diameter hole in both sides.

Next, align the bottom edges of the two sides then lay out the centered arched cutout. To do that, set your compass at 2½" then find the location where the compass hits the marks along the bottom edge (3¾" from the out-side edges) and 1¼" of height at the center – the compass point rests on the opposing workpiece when drawing the arch.

The photo above shows how to lay out the side's curved shape. Clamp a workpiece to your bench, clamp a thin strip of wood to the bench just in front of the work-piece then bend that strip to the 2⅞" layout mark along the top edge to get a pleasing shape. The radius of the line should be around 9¾".

With the strip bent to position, transfer the line to the side with a pencil. Use your jigsaw to cut close to the line and finish smoothing the curve with a rasp and sandpaper. This is the only time that you'll need to use this setup. The remaining layouts are transferred from this one curve.

A CHOICE OF POWER TOOLS

Align the sides to transfer the layout from the first side workpiece to the second side, then flip the shaped side and repeat to add the second curve to second side. There's one curve yet to add, but that comes after you shape the second side.

You could use a jigsaw to cut the curve to the final dimension, but a router with a pattern bit installed does the job in a flash – then rasp cleanup isn't necessary and final sanding is minimal.

Use a jigsaw to rough-cut and stay about ⅛" from the layout line. (This allows the bit to cut exactly to the line.) Fit the sanded curve to the rough-sawn curve, clamp the pieces to your bench so the clamps are out of the path of the router's base as the cut is made, and you're ready.

A flush-cut router bit with a top-mount bearing makes shaping the curves quick work, but the profile is only as good as the one copied.

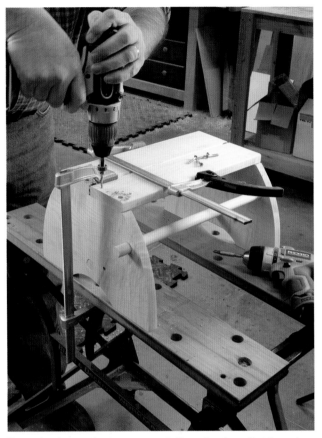

The seat boards, as are the steps, are spaced with pennies, clamped together and clamped to the frame prior to drilling for screws.

Adjust the router bit so the bearing rides along the sanded curve while the bit's cutting length is aligned to remove waste material. Make the cut moving the router from left to right, or with the direction the router bit is spinning. After routing the curve, flip the top board and repeat the steps to complete the work on that side.

Switch the sides then lay out, rough-cut and rout the remaining curved edge. The sides are complete after a bit of sanding.

If you want to bypass the router work, jigsaw, rasp and sand those three curved profiles.

There's a bit of layout and shaping work done to the step supports. Make sure to locate the ¼" holes prior to any shaping. The bottom edges of the supports have gentle curves and the corners are softened, or rounded. Make the cuts with your jigsaw, then use a rasp and sandpaper to finish the shaping. Or use the router setup to complete this work, like you did on the sides.

ON TO ASSEMBLY

The seat boards, with the edges rounded with a block plane, are taken from standard-width stock, but the steps need to be ripped to width. Use your jigsaw to make the cuts and clean the sawn edges with a block plane. Sand all the parts, including the dowels, to clean up the surfaces and you're ready to assemble.

Position the dowels: The short dowel fits toward the bottom center of the sides with the ends flush with the exterior face of the sides. The longer dowel acts as a stop when the step is flipped up and the stool is in seat mode. This dowel extends ¾" beyond the exterior faces of the sides. After the dowels are positioned, drill ⅛" cross holes through the edge of the sides and into the dowels. Glue in a dowel pin to secure everything.

The seat boards and the steps are attached with countersunk and piloted screws. Plug the screw holes then sand the areas smooth and it's time for finish, be it paint or stain and topcoats.

With the finish complete, attach the step support assembly to the main stool assembly using lag bolts, washers and nuts (slip an extra washer between the support and side to keep the parts separated) then take the stool into the house and watch your youngsters reach new heights.

CUTTING LIST

| NO. | PART | DIMENSIONS (T, W, L) | |
		INCHES	MILLIMETERS
2	Sides	¾ x 7¼ x 12½	19 x 184 x 318
2	Seatboards	¾ x 3½ x 16½	19 x 89 x 419
1	Long dowel	¾ dia. x 18	19 dia. x 457
1	Short dowel	¾ dia. x 16½	19 dia. x 419
2	Step supports	¾ x 3½ x 14½	19 × 89 x 369
4	Dowel pins	⅛ dia. x 2	3 dia. x 51
2	Steps	¾ x 2¼ x 18⅛	19 × 57 x 460

HARDWARE

2	Carriage bolts, ¼" × 2"	
2	Nuts, ¼"	
4	Washers, ¼"	

Side Elevation

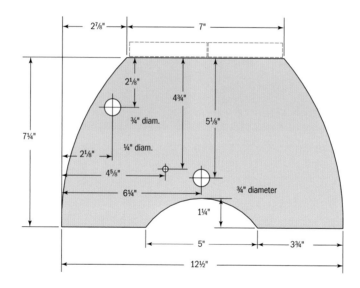

Support Arm

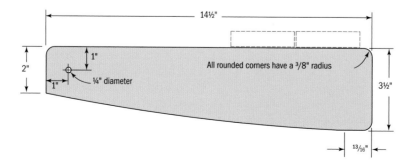

INDEX

ABOUT THE AUTHORS

STEVE BLENK
Steve was a contributing edtior for *American Woodworker* and *Woodworker's Journal* and author of numerous articles on woodturning.

TOM CASPAR
Tom is the former editor of *Woodwork* and *American Woodworker* magazines.

MEGAN FITZPATRICK
Megan is the editor of *Popular Woodworking Magazine.*

A.J. HAMLER
A.J. is the former editor of *Woodshop News* and the founding editor of *Woodcraft Magazine.* He is the author of numerous woodworking books including "Birdhouses & More" and "Build It With Dad."

GLEN D. HUEY
Glen is a former senior editor with *Popular Woodworking Magazine* and the author of several woodworking books.

JOCK HOLMEN
Jock has been a professional woodworker for more than 40 years and is a former contributing editor to *American Woodworker* magazine.

JOE HURST-WAJSZCZUK
Joe is the senior editor for *Woodcraft Magazine.*

RANDY JOHNSON
Randy is the former editor-in-chief for *American Woodworker* magazine. He is currently the Chief Operations Officer at ShopBot Tools.

AL KROGH
After working for 36 years in a large company, Al Krogh took early retirement from the corporate world in order to spend more time on his hobbies including designing and building children's furniture.

ALAN LACER
Alan has been involved in the woodturning field for more than 38 years as a turner, teacher writer and past president of the American Association of Woodturners.

TREVOR SMITH
Trevor is a physics teacher at Troy High School. He was introduced to woodworking in middle school woodshop. He now creates furniture pieces and wood turnings in his home workshop.

Making Classic Wooden Toys. Copyright © 2016 by
Popular Woodworking. Printed and bound in China. All
rights reserved. No part of this book may be reproduced
in any form or by any electronic or mechanical means
including information storage and retrieval systems
without permission in writing from the publisher, except
by a reviewer, who may quote brief passages in a review.
Published by Popular Woodworking Books, an imprint
of F+W Media, Inc., 10151 Carver Rd. Blue Ash, Ohio,
45242. (800) 289-0963. First edition.

Distributed in Canada by Fraser Direct
100 Armstrong Avenue
Georgetown, Ontario L7G 5S4
Canada

Distributed in the U.K. and Europe by
F+W Media International, LTD
Pynes Hill Court
Pynes Hill
Rydon Lane
Exeter
EX2 5SP
Tel: +44 1392 797680

Visit our website at popularwoodworking.com or our
consumer website at shopwoodworking.com for more
woodworking information projects.

Other fine Popular Woodworking Books are available
from your local bookstore or direct from the publisher.

ISBN-13: 978-1-4403-4763-4

20 19 18 17 16   5 4 3 2 1

Editor: Scott Francis
Designer: Laura Spencer
Production coordinator: Debbie Thomas

READ THIS IMPORTANT SAFETY NOTICE

To prevent accidents, keep safety in mind while you work. Use the safety guards installed on power equipment; they are for your protection.

When working on power equipment, keep fingers away from saw blades, wear safety goggles to prevent injuries from flying wood chips and sawdust, wear hearing protection and consider installing a dust vacuum to reduce the amount of airborne sawdust in your woodshop.

Don't wear loose clothing, such as neckties or shirts with loose sleeves, or jewelry, such as rings, necklaces or bracelets, when working on power equipment. Tie back long hair to prevent it from getting caught in your equipment.

People who are sensitive to certain chemicals should check the chemical content of any product before using it.

Due to the variability of local conditions, construction materials, skill levels, etc., neither the author nor Popular Woodworking Books assumes any responsibility for any accidents, injuries, damages or other losses incurred resulting from the material presented in this book.

The authors and editors who compiled this book have tried to make the contents as accurate and correct as possible. Plans, illustrations, photographs and text have been carefully checked. All instructions, plans and projects should be carefully read, studied and understood before beginning construction.

Prices listed for supplies and equipment were current at the time of publication and are subject to change.

METRIC CONVERSION CHART

TO CONVERT	TO	MULTIPLY BY
Inches	Centimeters	2.54
Centimeters	Inches	0.4
Feet	Centimeters	30.5
Centimeters	Feet	0.03
Yards	Meters	0.9
Meters	Yards	1.1

a content + ecommerce company

IDEAS · INSTRUCTION · INSPIRATION

Receive FREE downloadable bonus materials when you sign up
for our FREE newsletter at **popularwoodworking.com**.

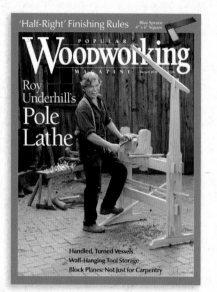

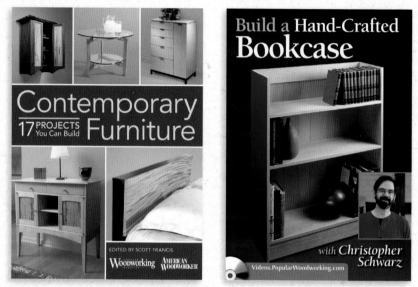

Find the latest issues of *Popular Woodworking Magazine* on newsstands, or visit **popularwoodworking.com**.

These and other great Popular Woodworking products are available at your local bookstore, woodworking store or online supplier. Visit our website at **shopwoodworking.com**.

Popular Woodworking Videos

Subscribe and get immediate access to the web's best woodworking subscription site. You'll find more than 400 hours of woodworking video tutorials and full-length video workshops from world-class instructors on workshops, projects, SketchUp, tools, techniques and more!

videos.popularwoodworking.com

Visit our Website

Find helpful and inspiring articles, videos, blogs, projects and plans at **popularwoodworking.com**.

 For behind the scenes information, become a fan at **Facebook.com/popularwoodworking**.

 For more tips, clips and articles, follow us at **twitter.com/pweditors**.

 For visual inspiration, follow us at **pinterest.com/popwoodworking**.

 For free videos visit **youtube.com/popwoodworking**.